D1272945

95

INSIDE THE NORTH YORK MOORS

INSIDE THE
NORTH YORK MOORS

HARRY MEAD

DAVID & CHARLES
Newton Abbot   London   North Pomfret (Vt)

To my wife
SHIRLEY
who endures me and the moors

British Library Cataloguing in Publication Data

Mead, Harry
    Inside the North York Moors.
    1. North York Moors, Eng. – Description and travel
    I. Title
    914.28'46'04857   DA670.Y6

ISBN 0–7153–7699–3

Library of Congress Catalog Card Number 78–62492

First published 1978
Second impression 1979

© Harry Mead 1978

All rights reserved. No part of this
publication may be reproduced, stored
in a retrieval system, or transmitted,
in any form or by any means, electronic,
mechanical, photocopying, recording or
otherwise, without the prior permission
of David & Charles (Publishers) Limited

Photoset and printed in Great Britain
by Redwood Burn Limited
Trowbridge & Esher
for David & Charles (Publishers) Limited
Brunel House Newton Abbot Devon

Published in the United States of America
by David & Charles Inc
North Pomfret Vermont 05053 USA

CONTENTS

CONTENTS

FOREWORD

This book is not meant to be a village by village, or even a valley by valley, guide to the North York Moors. I hope that by using the index the visitor will be able to pick out points of interest wherever he might be. By dealing with the region under subject headings I have been able to say more about a wide range of topics than would be possible by the alternative travelogue approach.

Even so, I am aware of loose ends that have not fitted neatly into my pattern and have had to be left aside. There will also be matters I have overlooked, or which I do not mention because I do not know of them—for learning about places like the moors is a process that lasts a lifetime. To anyone who feels I have done less than justice to a cherished corner, or have disregarded a favourite fragment of moorland history, I apologise.

Two broad omissions were intended at the outset. One is the principal monuments in the care of the Department of the Environment—Rievaulx Abbey, Helmsley Castle, etc. These crop up incidentally in the text and are shown on my map, but as they already draw visitors easily enough there seemed little point in duplicating the very thorough basic information available on the spot.

The other omission is the region's forests, for which, frankly, I do not greatly care. To me extensive conifer plantations smother the landscape, and while there is open moor and dappled English woodland you will rarely find me in the formal forests. To those who do not share my inhibitions perhaps I might mention here that the forest between Pickering and Scarborough contains a complex of drives and nature trails, with a 'visitor centre' at Low Dalby. Ask the whereabouts of a forest pool containing goldfish—an oddity in that region. For the next 18 years, up to 1990, the Forestry Commission will also be establishing a major arboretum at Dalby, in which every species of tree found in the forest will be represented.

I have not adhered rigidly to the official boundary of the national park, which in several places is far too tightly drawn. Few would deny, for instance, that Kirkdale and St Gregory's Minster, excluded from the park, amply deserve to be in it. I have also thought it proper to make occasional sallies into some of the towns bordering the park, particularly Whitby and Helmsley, major centres for visitors to the moors and whose history and character are in tune with the region.

I can state precisely the moment when the special beauty and strength of the moors first struck deeply home to me. It came as I travelled westwards one November evening in 1967 after a visit to Robin Hood's Bay for my work. The dark mass of the moors rolled away to merge into a tremendous November sunset. Alone in my car I might have been alone on a planet of moor. In my experience only the moors, among many magnificent kinds of countryside, afford so strong a sense of infinity, which it does us all good to be reminded of from time to time.

Since that memorable evening the moors have been my landscape. The hope behind this book is that they will become yours too.

Harry Mead
Great Broughton
near Stokesley
1978

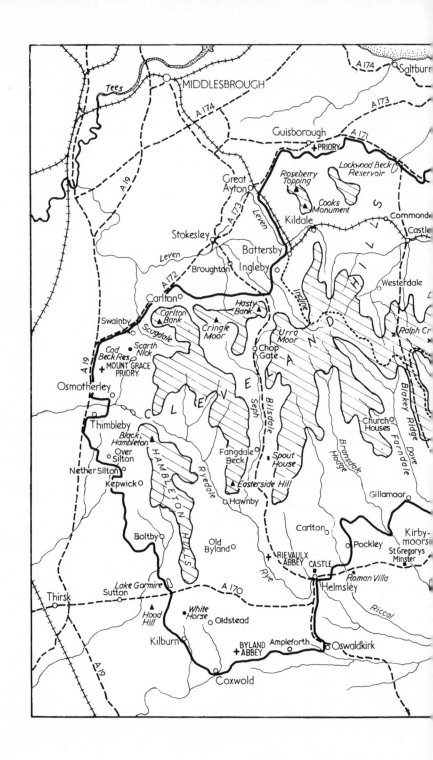

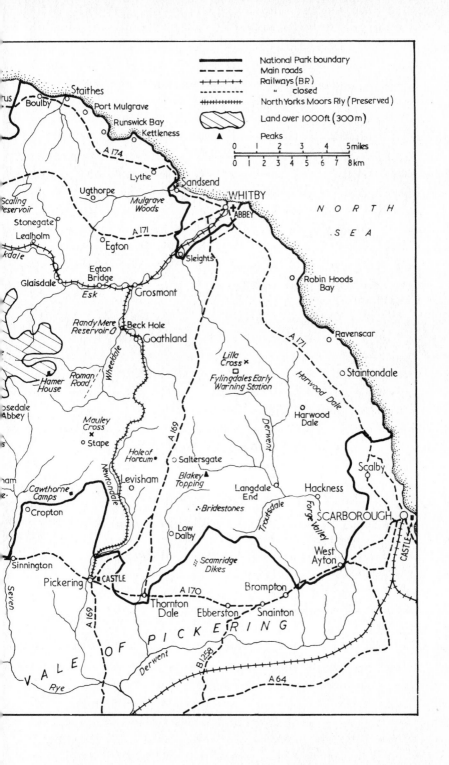

1

A LIVING LANDSCAPE

How the Heather Came

Pick up almost any book about North Yorkshire and you are
soon likely to read of the 'rolling heather moorlands'. When the
North York Moors became a National Park in 1952 an official
brochure promptly declared: 'The real attraction is acres of
open moor stretching to the horizon and in August and September ablaze with the purple flower of the heather . . .' But
there is another way of viewing this scenic masterpiece—as a
monument to man, the ravager, over the last 10,000 years.

It was once widely believed that the heather spread rapidly
across the moors immediately after the Ice Age. This opinion is
found in a classic study, *The Moorlands of North-East Yorkshire*, by
Frank Elgee, published in 1912. But it has more recently been
established that the heather did not arrive until long after the
departure of the ice. Some interesting work was carried out between 1962 and 1970 by the Geography Department of
Durham University. Taking core samples through the moorland peat, which has accumulated in depths of up to 35ft since
the Ice Age, the team confirmed that the first significant vegetation was low scrub—mainly birch and juniper intermixed
with pine.

The shelter provided by these trees enabled other species to
gain a foothold. As the climate improved the newcomers became more dominant, and by about 8000bc the moors were
covered with a dense forest. Oak, birch, hazel, and elm were the

principal trees, but willow, beech and lime also flourished.

It was at this moment that man appeared—and the transformation he has wrought was neatly embodied in a core sample taken by the Durham team on Blakey Ridge. In the bottom layers of the peat between 80 and 90 per cent of preserved pollen grains were from trees, but in the top layer the picture was almost exactly reversed, with less than a quarter of the grains being from trees and the rest from heather, moss and grass. How this change occurred is the story of man on the moors.

The first known inhabitants of North Yorkshire were hunters of the Middle Stone Age or Mesolithic period. Some of Britain's best evidence of these people came when the remains of former lakeside dwellings were found in 1949 at Starr Carr near Seamer, south of Scarborough. Although this settlement was on lowland, the hunters probably burned parts of the forest to flush out game and to create clearings in which to catch their prey. There is some evidence that towards the end of this period semi-permanent camps may have been established in the clearings.

During the next period, the New Stone Age beginning about 3000BC, further inroads were made as the forest accommodated man's first attempts at cultivation. But the Durham research suggests that away from the newly tilled plots the forest may have recovered some lost ground.

In about 1700BC, however, the nomadic people of the Bronze Age began the first of two great clearances of the forest. Living off their animals they gradually colonised the whole of the moor tops. Never before or since has the moorland plateau been 'home' to so many people. The grazing of their cattle, sheep and goats prevented the forest from renewing itself, and although the valleys remained thickly wooded the high moors became largely denuded of trees. As rainwater steadily washed the goodness from the soil, hazel scrub replaced the tall forest trees and in turn gave way to moorland grasses. Today these grasses can be seen fighting a losing battle with the heather, which is virtually all that the thin, acid soil of the high moors will now support.

14

But even a thousand years of relentless grazing by the animals of the Bronze Age did not bring the open panorama of today's moors fully into being. Incredibly, some woodland survived—only to be attacked when the Iron Age people needed fuel for their primitive furnaces, or as they cleared ground in the search for ore. More trees were felled by the Vikings and Romans, but the second great clearance of the woodland was destined to come from a more surprising quarter—monks!

The Durham research indicates that even on the tops a few scattered remnants of the forest stood until about AD 1200. They were erased by the great sheep runs of the new monasteries. And while their sheep grazed the hills, the monks or their lay brothers set about cultivating the valleys, until then ill drained and largely uninhabitable. When the monastic age closed in the sixteenth century the moor-and-dale scenery that we know today was virtually complete except for the field enclosures carried out mainly in the seventeenth and eighteenth centuries.

It is a mistake, however, to regard today's moors as either 'changeless' or a 'wilderness'—the terms probably most often applied to them. Since the nineteenth century the heather has been carefully managed as a crop for grouse: controlled burning, undertaken outside the breeding season, encourages the young shoots on which the birds like to feed. Even areas of bog can have commercial value, for nurserymen at Pickering pack their plants in sponge-like sphagnum moss harvested from the moors. During World War I large quantities of the moss were sent to France as an absorbent substitute for scarce cotton wool!

The open moorland is now struggling for survival. Between 1950 and 1975 its share of the national park shrank from about half to just over 40 per cent. The lost acres were claimed mostly by forestry or the plough, and it has been gloomily calculated that if these trends continue unabated there will be no moorland at all in about 150 years' time.

That outcome is perhaps unlikely, and for the moment there is no exaggeration in claims about a forty-mile carpet of heather stretching from the Vale of York to the sea. In common with that early national park brochure, most tourist literature directs attention to the moorland vista when the heather is in bloom. The spectacle is indeed breathtaking. But the moors are magnificent in all seasons, and their appeal grows with closer acquaintance of their many moods. I find them most impressive at dusk in late autumn or early winter, when the moorland horizon merging into the darkening sky creates the effect of a world filled with moor—a humbling experience.

Only a year or two ago I was at a picnic spot on the edge of the moors when an American visitor came up to me and asked, 'Do you have any moors around here?' I was able to direct his party to the road between Kildale and Westerdale, which I believe offers the finest introduction to the moorland scenery. Moors of many shapes and sizes heave on all sides, rising from the bright green valleys that form the perfect setting to the often sombre crown. The value of such landscapes as a source of personal enrichment, whether you are tramping across them or merely looking at them, is impossible to assess.

Lions at Kirkdale

Tucked into a fold of the moors between Helmsley and Kirbymoorside is the sheltered glade of Kirkdale. A church (see St Gregory's Minster, p 141), a ford and a footbridge contribute to a scene of quiet charm. And high in the wooded cliff overlooking it all is the narrow opening of Kirkdale Cave, a place with an astonishing story to tell.

Workmen quarrying roadstone in March 1821 broke into the cave and stumbled on evidence that Britain was once the natural home of the lion, the tiger, the rhinoceros, the hippopotamus and many other now alien creatures. The evidence was a large quantity of animal bones and teeth. But the workmen did not at first realise the significance of their find, and it was only when a local doctor, John Harrison, noticed unusual fragments of bone among the stone scattered on local roads that the truth emerged.

Altogether twenty-two species of animal were identified. Dated broadly at 70,000BC, they cover a huge span of time culminating in the onset of the last Ice Age. The relics of lion, tiger and hippo, and of other animals such as the bison, the straight-tusked elephant, the giant deer and the slender-nosed rhino, indicate that at the beginning of the period Britain was a warm country, perhaps even sub-tropical. A primeval forest would have covered much of the land—quite different from the English woodland that developed after the Ice Age. But by the end of the period Britain had become a cold steppe, its forest replaced by tundra waste. The remains of a mammoth were from that time, and his companions at Kirkdale included the woolly rhino and the reindeer.

From the large number of hyena bones—more than 300, excluding others known to have been thrown away by the roadmen—it is believed that the cave was a hyenas' den into which the scavengers had dragged the carcases of other animals. The failure to find any complete skeleton in the cave also points to the hyena, which devours even its own dead. The cave also contained what a contemporary report described as 'many small balls of the solid calcareous excrement of an animal that fed on bone'—another feature of the diet of the hyena.

An early puzzle was the discovery of a thick layer of sediment. At one time this was awesomely attributed to the biblical flood. But geologists are now confident the mud was deposited by the waters of Lake Pickering, a tremendous lake created by glaciers in and around the moors (see p 18). Reaching a height of 250ft above sea level the lake would have totally submerged the Kirkdale Cave at 175ft.

The most puzzling feature of the cave today is its entrance—8ft wide but only 3ft high. Originally it was 11ft by 5ft, but it decreased in size as the roadmen continued their work. The present letter-box-like opening makes it hard to believe that the cave contains four branch-passages, including two places in which an adult can stand up. Local people say that the cave is part of a wide system, and tell the story of a goose that made its way underground from Kirkdale to Kirbymoorside, but in doing so lost all of its feathers.

Still unresolved is the question of whether the hyenas were forced from the cave by the rising waters of Lake Pickering or whether they left before the water arrived because of the changing climate. But it is very unlikely that any human being ever witnessed the doubtless amazing scenes around the cave. The hunters of Starr Carr, near Scarborough, the first known men in the region, did not appear until the close of the Ice Age. By that time Kirkdale Cave had almost certainly been abandoned for centuries. The lion would no longer roar in the North Yorkshire forests, nor the hippo wallow in the warm waters of Ryedale.

A Vanished Lakeland

From the southern slopes of the North York Moors, the Vale of Pickering is often veiled in a delicate blue haze, like a sheet of water covering the plain. It is then that Yorkshire's vanished lakeland can easily be imagined to have reappeared.

An immense lake, much larger than any now found in England, once occupied almost the whole of the vale. The horseshoe arrangement of towns and principal villages around the edge of the vale is a reminder that this fertile stretch of countryside was a marsh within historic times.

There were other lakes as well—in Eskdale, Glaisdale and Scugdale, and at Wheeldale, Hackness, Kildale and Fen Bog. The latter impressively matches its name and survives as the last remnant of an extensive swamp that existed after all the lakes drained away.

The lakes were formed as a result of the Ice Age that began to grip North Yorkshire about 70,000 years ago. The period lasted about 60,000 years, and the changes it caused have made the moors a classic area in Britain for the study of glaciation.

Three glaciers converged on the district—from the North Sea, Scotland, and the Lake District. They were not thick enough to overtop the highest moorland, but they pressed on the edges and up the valleys. The moor road between Whitby and Guisborough for several miles defines the limit of the north Sea ice. On the seaward side is farmland, on boulder clay deposited by the glacier. On the other side lie the impoverished soils of the high moors.

A glance at the map also shows that near Scarborough the River Derwent advances to within $1\frac{1}{2}$ miles of the sea. It then swings abruptly south, beginning a 90 mile detour that takes it to the sea via the Humber. The Derwent originally flowed directly to the coast, but it became blocked by the North Sea ice. To this the moors owe the attractive Forge Valley—the route carved by the Derwent on a new course to the Vale of Pickering.

But before the new course was cut, water piled up to form Hackness Lake. At the same time, the North Sea ice, pressing up the Esk Valley and its tributaries, created further natural dams at Lealholm, Glaisdale, and Goathland. The water thus trapped became the lakes of Eskdale, Glaisdale, and Wheeldale.

The North Sea glacier also swept in from Teesmouth to the moors around Stokesley. On the western flank of Cold Moor you can collect pebbles of the Norwegian rock rhomb porphry, probably marking the limit of the glacier's penetration. More obviously, the glacier dumped a massive moraine, now a giant wooded embankment, at Dundale Beck, near Kildale. By damming the River Leven this caused Kildale Lake to appear, perhaps uniting with Lake Eskdale in places. Not far away, the Scottish glacier created Lake Scugdale by throwing a wall of ice across a small valley near Swainby.

Meanwhile, the Lake District glacier clamped itself against the escarpment bordering the Vale of York. Blocking the gap between Coxwold and Ampleforth it thereby cut off the western exit of the Vale of Pickering. With the eastern end barred by the North Sea ice near Brompton, the Vale, which lies between the North York Moors and the Yorkshire Wolds, became totally enclosed. The huge quantities of water pouring in formed Lake Pickering, 32 miles long and between 4 and 8 miles wide.

The ice melted in a thaw that began about 22,000 years ago

19

and lasted about 10,000 years. Along the Vale of York the water eddying between the glacier and the moors probably shaped the conical Hood Hill and influenced the formation of Lake Gormire (see p 216). At Scugdale the water overflowing from the glacial lake wore a shallow channel on Whorlton Moor. As the ice retreated from the mouth of this dale the lake increased in size. Its level dropped below that of the overflow channel, which thus became dry. About half a mile long and about 50yd wide and 25ft deep the channel can be found on the western rim of the valley.

With the wall of ice standing back from the hills, the Scugdale water worked round to the front of the Cleveland escarpment. There it escaped by carving another channel, above Swainby. Named Scarth Nick and accommodating the road from Swainby to Osmotherley, this channel is a distinct V-shaped gap, a landmark from many miles to the north.

The Esk system outdid even these effects. The lakes of Eskdale, Glaisdale, and Wheeldale all drained to Fen Bog. They, too, cut overflow channels that now appear as dry beds. Between Key Green, near Egton Bridge, and Goathland are a whole series: Moss Swang, Ewe Crag Slack, Lady Bridge Slack, and Park Dyke Slack. They lie parallel but at different heights, indicating stages in the retreat of the ice. The largest of the channels, Park Dyke, is partly occupied by Randy Mere, a reservoir for Whitby. Almost totally surrounded by trees, the reservoir can be glimpsed briefly from the road between Egton Bridge and Goathland. It has an unusual claim to fame as one of the last places in England where leeches were gathered. In 1945 an elderly Goathland resident recalled how he collected the leeches many years earlier by wading into the mere and allowing the creatures to attach themselves to his skin. Not far from the mere, in the same dry channel and also visible from the road, is a neatly cut peat pit, worked by a householder from Darnholm.

The tremendous volume of water at Fen Bog soon spilled southwards into Newton Dale, which is one of the most dramatic features of the moors. The tiny stream trickling through

20

the dale today could not possibly have cut a valley on this scale, with cliffs up to 400ft high. What did so were the escaping waters of the Esk's glacier system, thundering and boiling through the dale for thousands of years. Beneath the soil, south of Pickering, lies confirmation of the cataract—an extensive fan-shaped deposit of gravel, left by the torrent as it entered Lake Pickering.

For its part, the great lake could hardly accept this crescendo of water without offering a reply. It did so by cutting its own impressive escape route, Kirkham Gorge, through the wolds south of Malton.

Back in the moors nothing could be the same again. When the ice disappeared the Derwent was securely fixed in its new course. The Esk, however, aimed straight for the sea. After slicing through the glacial clays it began a fantastic attack on the underlying rock, cutting ten gorges in its final 12 miles to Whitby. The narrowness of these gorges explains why roads in this part of the district do not follow the valley floor but switchback up and down a series of severe hills. Railway builders were undeterred, however, and between Lealholm and Whitby the local passenger line crosses the Esk seventeen times. Although probably few people realise it, the railway journey here, in common with that down glacial Newton Dale, puts the visitor in touch with momentous events in the making of the moors.

Marks of Man

The longest earthwork in the North York Moors runs like a furrowed scar for almost three miles along a flank of the hills enclosing the head of Bilsdale. Starting at crags near Clay Bank it holds a remarkably level course at about 1,100ft, swerving into and out of a tiny valley before fading near William Beck Farm beyond Chop Gate. No one knows what it was for.

Part of the fascination of the moors is that they contain many echoes of the far-distant past. Some of the marks of man on the moors go back almost to the beginnings of our civilisation. The moors are thus one of the few landscapes preserving

21

this important link. And for the moorland walker there is always the opportunity to strike across the heather to some seldom visited example of man's early handiwork—and ponder what it was all about.

Oddly, the Bilsdale earthwork might not be all that old. A local theory is that this massive ditch and rampart was put up to repel William the Conqueror during his harrying of the North. There is a legend that William got lost in a snowstorm on the Bilsdale moors. Some people say there was once a phrase in Bilsdale, 'swearing like Billy Norman', though I have yet to hear any dalesman use it. But a claim that the valley is named after William I (Bill's Dale!) is not as fanciful as might be supposed, for the word Bilsdale is based on the old Norse personal name 'Bildr'. The first written record, in the twelfth century, is Byldesdale.

It is unlikely, however, that Bilsdale people could have raised so impressive an earthwork to meet William's relatively sudden invasion. The rampart is up to 12ft wide and 9ft high. Dry-stone walling is visible, at one point rising to twelve courses. A possible purpose of the earthwork was to mark a boundary between the territories of the abbeys at Rievaulx and Kirkham. Rievaulx's records mention 'land below the dike', and it could be that the dike enclosed a deer park. This belief is reinforced by a thatched building known as West Park that once stood near the dike at Orra. It collapsed in the 1960s.

Other moors present other mysteries. On Danby High Moor are more than 800 hummocks, consisting almost entirely of small stones. These were formerly regarded as prehistoric burials, but excavations have produced nothing to support this theory. A similar group of about 300 mounds, apparently linked by about 1¼ miles of primitive stone walling, can be seen on Cow Ridge, Snilesworth. A fairly recent suggestion is that the stones were scraped together as the ground was cleared for early attempts at cultivation. In the Welsh mountains, however, groups of stony cairns are found at heights of more than 2,000ft, beyond the limit of cultivation. So the puzzle remains.

In the south of the national park, speculation surrounds the

finest enclosure-type of earthwork in the district—Studfold or
Studford Ring near Ampleforth. The ring is 54yd in diameter,
with a rampart 24ft wide, and a 9ft wide entrance. Immediately
inside is a ditch about 12ft wide and 4ft deep. Excavations have
been fruitless, but a smaller circle on Great Ayton Moor has
yielded fragments of Iron Age pottery. This has encouraged a
belief that the ring was an Iron Age compound for horses and
cattle which increased in importance during the period. A shallow bank runs from the ring, and this might have been the
boundary of land cultivated by the community that used the
compound. Away to the west are a series of double dikes that
perhaps formed an outer defence.

Almost certainly built for defence is an unusual earthwork
running between two outcrops of crags on Horn Nab, Farndale.
A man-made bank appears to have been encased in large
stones—an ambitious task. Old local explanations are that it
was put up either against raiders in the Norman period or as a
rifle range in the Boer War. It almost certainly predates the
latter conflict, but not a single relic has been found there. Some
people suggest that the threat that led to the creation of the
defence perhaps never materialised, so the fortification might
have been manned only intermittently over a relatively short
period, rather like the pill boxes of World War II.

Of course, not everything is guesswork. Many moors are
surmounted by pork-pie-like mounds known as howes. The
largest of these have names: Simon Howe, Shunner Howe, etc.
They have long been known to be the burial places of the
ubiquitous Bronze Age people. There is a theory that these
nomads compensated for their lack of permanent homes by
making their burial grounds places of size and splendour. On
Loose Howe in 1937 Frank Elgee (see p 40) uncovered what
had obviously been a very important burial, probably of a
chief. The body lay in a canoe, with a second canoe as a lid and
a third alongside. The vessels had curved prows and slots for a
rudder. Together with other relics from the burial, including
the remains of leggings, shoes, a skin-cloak and a knife, they
are now in the care of the British Museum—and each year the

boots of many thousand Lyke Wake walkers tramp over the place where they were found.

Although now legally protected, the howes have not always enjoyed such respect. Behind the Lion Inn on Blakey Ridge is a howe that was long ago scooped out and robbed. Its name, Cockpit Howe, indicates its popular use. (Another possible cockpit was at the impressive group of rocks known as Low Cable Stones, Tripsdale, off Bilsdale. Some people believe that a prehistoric rock shelter might also have existed there.)

Notable discoveries continue to be made. In 1969 a bulldozer making a Forestry Commission car park at Clay Bank, near Great Broughton, exposed a Bronze Age cemetery and crematorium. A stone flue bore signs of heavy burning and contained charcoal, charred fragments of bone and a clinker that could have been food. At least one of the eight dead had been a child, and from the shape of certain bones it seemed that another person had suffered rickets when young. The car park is now very popular, and it seems a pity that no plaque has been put up to explain the site's history.

Easily the most extensive of man's early efforts on the moors are the Scamridge Dikes, occupying almost 3 square miles north of Ebberston, near Pickering. Although not now easy to delineate among forestry and farmland, the dikes are a series of roughly parallel mounds and ditches, deep enough in places to conceal a man on horseback. Their north–south lay-out suggests that they were constructed as a defence against invaders from the sea. About 100 years ago they were one of Britain's most abundant sources of flint arrow-heads and other prehistoric weapons, and there seems no good reason to abandon the conclusion reached in 1905 by Gordon Home in his book *Pickering: The Evolution of an English Town*, in which he says: 'There can be little doubt that the dikes were the scene of great inter-tribal struggles if the loss of such infinite quantities of weapons is to be adequately accounted for.'

King Alfred of Northumbria is said to have taken refuge in a cave at Ebberston after a battle on Scamridge Dikes in AD705. The cave is no longer there, but on the summit of the crag where it used to be is a stone shelter commemorating the battle. The shelter was erected by Sir Charles Hotham in 1790.

The oldest man-made structures in the national park are a handful of 'long barrows', burial mounds of the New Stone Age, dating from between 3,000 and 5,000 years ago. Examination of two of the barrows, at Scamridge and Kepwick, revealed a jumbled mass of bones, which at one time were taken as evidence of cannibalism. Although this view is now distrusted no satisfactory alternative explanation has yet been put forward.

One curious instance of the imprint of man not being all it seems is provided by a series of rectangular mounds on a bankside at Hutton-le-Hole. People who dig there hoping to find evidence of an ancient past are bound to be disappointed, for the mounds are a rare example of a man-made rabbit warren, probably no more than 200 years old. Landowners sometimes created attractive burrowing places for rabbits, which were then trapped or shot. The Hutton-le-Hole warren probably belonged to nearby Douthwaite Hall, serving as a game reserve comparable to the more familiar fish pond or pigeon cote.

The Moorland Crosses

When a competition was held to select an official symbol for the North York Moors National Park most people were pleased that the final choice turned out to be a lonely moorland cross. For not only do the moors contain Britain's largest concentration of old stone crosses, but the crosses seem particularly at home in the moorland landscape.

Altogether there are more than thirty named crosses in the district. Some are no more than a stump or socket-stone, and a few have vanished completely though still named on maps. But enough complete crosses exist to attract the attention of most visitors.

The oldest moorland cross is probably Lilla, easily reached on foot from Ellerbeck Bridge on the Whitby–Pickering road. Believed to date from the seventh century, it is often said to be the oldest Christian monument in the North of England. It marks the grave of Lilla, chief minister to King Edwin of Deira, an ancient British kingdom centred on the wolds. When an attempt was made to stab Edwin, Lilla flung himself between the king and the would-be assassin, dying on the double-edged poisoned dagger. This attack is said to have taken place in Edwin's palace at either Malton or Aldby-by-Buttercrambe.

When Fylingdales Moor became a military training ground in 1952, Lilla Cross was moved for safety to the edge of the Whitby–Pickering road. But ten years later a Sandsend man, Graham Leach, arranged for its return to Lilla Howe. The work was carried out by a group of Sappers from the 508 Field Squadron, Horden, County Durham. The first task was the construction of a special cradle, in which the cross was transported to Horden for the removal of $1\frac{1}{2}$ tons of unwanted cement on its base. The Sappers, miners in daily life, completed this work and re-erected the cross on Lilla Howe without the slightest damage to the 1,300-year-old relic.

Most of the crosses were probably put up as waymarkers in the Middle Ages. Although plain guideposts would no doubt have done just as well, crosses were probably chosen because they served as a reminder of Christ, a comfort to the traveller crossing the desolate waste. In a booklet published by the Whitby Literary and Philosophical Society, T. H. Woodwark quotes a 1496 treatise on the Ten Commandments which says: 'For this reason ben crosses by ye waye, that when folke passynge see the crosses they sholde think on Hym that deyed on the cross and worshype Hym above all thynge.' Besides crossroads, favourite sites for the crosses were the entrances to villages and the junction of parishes. Woodwark claims that some crosses might have been put up to mark a notable event, such as a murder. Many crosses became convenient points for farmers and pedlars.

The cross selected as the national park symbol is Ralph Cross, by the roadside on Blakey Ridge between Castleton and Hutton-le-Hole. This shapely cross has a nick in the top into which passers-by used to place coins for more needy travellers. This custom was probably observed at other crosses, and its origin could lie in the Roman practice of offering food and drink to a local spirit. A hint of this is contained in a rhyme about the now vanished Cropton Cross:

> On Cropton Cross there is a cup
> And in that cup there is a sup
> Take that cup and drink that sup
> And put that cup on Cropton Cross.

Some people still put money in Ralph Cross, and in 1961 the shaft snapped as a local man climbed to recover the coins. Scars on the cross indicate where the three broken sections were skilfully grafted together. Unfortunately, however, only three months after the repair was completed the whole cross tilted in a gale and more work had to be carried out.

Ralph Cross is often erroneously called 'Ralph's Cross'. To give him his full Sunday title he is 'Young Ralph'. An elderly companion, Old Ralph, stands about 200yd to the west. Old Ralph is only 5ft high compared with Young Ralph's 9ft, but he enjoys a view of the sea! He is positioned on a ridgeway dividing Esklets, Westerdale and Rosedale, and a cross in that vicinity is mentioned in Guisborough charters of 1200. Young Ralph probably arrived when a change was made in the line of the moorland road in the eighteenth century.

Only a short distance from both these crosses—along the road to Rosedale—is a third well known cross, Fat Betty. She owes her name to her shape: a sturdy base surmounted only by the top of a wheelhead cross. A coat of whitewash completes the strong resemblance to a well scrubbed washerwoman. She marks the junction of the parishes of Danby, Westerdale and Rosedale.

Several tales are told about this trio of crosses. In one story, Young Ralph was a Danby man who died in a blizzard. Local people also used to say that the world would end when three kings met at Ralph Cross. Still often mentioned is a prophecy that when Young Ralph and Fat Betty meet there will be a wedding. But perhaps the best story is the one in which Old Ralph

27

is a Rosedale man, hired to accompany the prioresses of the Rosedale and Baysdale Abbeys on a tour of the moors to resolve a boundary dispute. The women got lost in dense fog, but Old Ralph found Sister Betty by the cross that now bears her name and Sister Margery by a large upright stone ever afterwards known as the Margery Stone. Old Ralph reunited the women where his cross now stands. The Margery Stone, incidentally, now marks the junction of the Lyke Wake Walk and Blakey Ridge.

In October 1971 these crosses and 11 others were linked in a 53-mile circular walk, pioneered by 6 men from the Scarborough–Malton area. On a hot weekend the following summer, 145 walkers took part in the first annual Crosses Walk. With scope for individual variation, the circuit is now a firmly established part of the moorland itinerary, though not all of it lies on rights of way and walkers should select their route with care. Among complete crosses visited on the walk are Mauley Cross near Stape, named after the de Mauley's of Mulgrave, and the 12ft Ainhowe Cross in Rosedale, probably put up in the nineteenth century to replace the ancient Ana Cross, the remains of which are in Lastingham Church.

I believe the late A. J. Brown best captured the atmosphere of the old stone crosses when he wrote that they 'imbue the moorlands with a strange religious solemnity not found elsewhere'. The crosses often seem to be an organic part of the moors, emphasising the deeply elemental feel of the landscape.

2

SOME CHARACTERS

'Mouseman' Thompson

Sometimes cleverly concealed and at others on view for all to see, a mouse each year attracts thousands of visitors to the North York Moors' village of Kilburn, near Thirsk. He appears on every item of furniture produced in the workshops founded by Robert Thompson, Yorkshire's celebrated 'mouseman'.

It is doubtful if there has ever been a more successful craft-industry emblem than the Thompson mouse. Thompson's brilliance as a woodcarver was probably bound to bring him recognition. But from the moment he carved his first mouse his eventual fame was assured. Any visit to the Kilburn showroom will confirm that among the people looking around, admiration for the beautifully made furniture, all of English oak, is mixed about equally with the serious business of 'spotting the mouse'. Almost everyone is on the lookout for him, perhaps finding him peering quizzically between leaves on a wall-light bracket, or dashing boldly up a grandfather clock—the mouse was Thompson's stroke of genius.

Thompson was born at Kilburn on 7 May 1876. His father was a joiner, wheelwright and builder. Like many Victorians, Mr Thompson was excited by the Industrial Revolution, and hence young Robert was sent to Cleckheaton as an engineering apprentice. But his father's premature death soon brought him home, to run the family business with his brothers William and Jack. They continued in their father's all-round tradition, and Robert was particularly involved in building Kilburn's village hall and the vicarage at nearby Husthwaite.

Some people who knew Thompson claim that his interest in woodcarving stemmed from visits he made to Ripon Cathedral while travelling to and from Cleckheaton. But when he left the family partnership to start a business of his own, he at first chose to be a stonemason. He opened a yard at York, employing three men. Husthwaite's World War I memorial is a reminder of the enterprise.

But by this time, Thompson was also an accomplished woodcarver. The earliest known example of his public work is the pulpit in Yearsley Church, near Helmsley, dating from 1907. People who seek it out look in vain for the mouse. No one knows when Thompson adopted the symbol, but it is unlikely to have been much before 1927, when Thompson registered the mouse as his trademark.

The Kilburn showroom incorporates part of Thompson's former home. Carved on the gleaming oak mantlepiece is a good example of his 'early mouse': it is raised on its forelegs and sports three-dimensional whiskers. Thompson soon discovered that this version of the mouse was easily damaged, and he accordingly set the mouse on its stomach, with its whiskers flat against its head.

Framed in the showroom are various envelopes that illustrate the pulling power of Thompson's brainchild. An envelope from Sydney, Australia, bears only a drawing of a mouse and the words 'Woodcarver, England'—but it reached Robert Thompson at Kilburn.

Oddly, however, Thompson's first great turning–point came before he introduced the mouse. Soon after World War I, Father Paul Nevill, headmaster of Ampleforth College, invited Thompson to make a new cross for the churchyard, after hearing of his skill from Mr Sydney Mawer, of Kilburn. Still virtually unknown beyond his village, Thompson selected an oak tree from a nearby estate. It was hauled by horses to his yard and hand-sawn over an open pit. Father Nevill was so impressed with the completed cross that he asked Thompson to make a chair and a table. Eventually Thompson did much more work at the college, most notably furnishing the magnificent library.

What led to the mouse? Several stories are told, the most

common of which is that Thompson chose the creature to represent 'industry in quiet places'. But in a letter to a Gloucestershire clergyman in 1949 Thompson gave a different account. Apparently, the idea came to him while he and a fellow workman were carving the cornice for a large church screen. When his companion mentioned the phrase 'as poor as a church mouse', Thompson commented that they were both as poor as mice, and it immediately crossed his mind that the mouse would make an attractive symbol. He carved his first mouse then and there, but unfortunately no one knows for which church the work was done.

Thompson's mouse adorns the candlesticks on the high altar in Westminster Abbey, and, as you would expect, it is found in several places in York Minster. Particularly interesting is the mouse on the archbishop's throne. A member of the Thompson family once told me that when Thompson was making the throne, a senior churchman objected to the mouse and said he would have it removed if Thompson included it. Thompson outwitted him by carving a niche in the throne, with the mouse curled tightly inside. It would be impossible to remove this inset mouse without seriously scarring the throne.

Thompson's original workshop, in use until the mid-1920s, stands almost opposite the present showroom. Thompson worked right up to his death in 1955, when the business passed to his only child, a daughter. It is now energetically carried on by Thompson's two grandsons, Robert and Jack Cartwright. The workforce has increased from thirty-five to about fifty since Thompson's death, and the sawn trunks of English oak, seasoning in the open air, are a more prominent feature of the village than ever.

Some visitors are surprised to see machines in the workshop. But Thompson himself recognised that certain tasks in furniture-making could be done as well by machine as by hand. He installed a number of machines, driven by a ramshackle network of belts that put visitors in fear of their lives. The few machines present today are used mainly for simple turning—and the standards of individual craftsmanship remain very high. On my last visit, for instance, I noticed a unique mouse, carved on the oak base of a bronze bust of Thompson. With its head emerging from a hole on one side of the base while its hindquarters disappeared on another, it gave the appearance of having nibbled its way through the block. The work of a present-day woodcarver, this playful piece of inspiration was worthy of 'the mouseman' himself.

Scugdale Giant

Henry Cooper is believed to have been born in Swainby, and as a boy he worked at Scugdale Hall Farm. An 1890 directory of the North Riding states that 'this remarkable sample of humanity grew thirteen inches in the space of five months'. It adds that Cooper's current height was 8ft 6in. He was at that time reputedly the world's tallest man, and if the evidence of the directory is admitted, he is easily the tallest-ever Englishman, beating the champion in the *Guinness Book of Records* (another Yorkshireman!) by 9in.

Cooper was certainly too tall for work on the farm: he couldn't move easily in the farm buildings, and he found it backbreaking to follow the plough. Dismissed by his employer, he travelled to London where he joined a circus. In the 1880s he toured the USA with Barnum and Bailey.

Visitors to the circus were sometimes photographed alongside Cooper. But although the aim was to show the giant's height, Cooper nevertheless sat down. The reason for this is said to have been that the photographer could not fit the group into his plates at an acceptable distance with Cooper standing.

Cooper married a tall woman from the circus, and when he returned to England he styled himself Sir Henry Alexander Cooper. But his unnatural height was probably associated with other abnormalities, for he died at the early age of thirty-two.

Sleights Forger

The son of a Whitby tailor, Edward Simpson was born in 1815. After gaining an insight into geology and archaeology while working for the Whitby historian Dr George Young, he began selling fossils and shells, which he collected on the seashore. In 1843 someone asked him if he could make a flint arrowhead. His first attempt, using a geologist's hammer, was a failure. But when he was idly chipping a piece of flint with the worn hasp of a gate, he found he could easily obtain very fine flakes. By carefully trimming these and gumming them together with boiled alum he produced masterly imitations of prehistoric arrowheads, which he sold as genuine at the rate of up to fifty a day.

In 1844 Simpson disposed of 600 worthless flints to one Bridlington dealer alone. Quickly nicknamed Flint Jack he extended his range. A particularly notable fake was of an ancient British urn, which he claimed he had unearthed on the moors between Stokesley and Kirbymoorside.

Outwardly open and honest, and to some people seeming even gullible, Simpson operated with much guile. He produced most of his fakes in a hut deep in the moors, at that time very little visited. Understanding the risk of swamping the Yorkshire market he moved to London, where he pulled off a scoop by selling a sham Roman milestone to the British Museum!

Simpson now judged the moment right to return to Yorkshire. At first he traded honestly in fossils and shells, and even when he reverted to the more profitable fakes, he prudently sold most of them in County Durham.

But Simpson's dishonesty eventually caught up with him. A Bridlington dealer decided to boil some of Flint Jack's arrowheads because they were dirtier than others in his collection. When the flints were bleached white their splinter composition was clearly revealed.

Simpson slipped away to London, but news of his trickery quickly reached the capital. The reaction of those who had been deceived was astonishing. They agreed not to press charges if Flint Jack would demonstrate his skill, which he did before a gathering of scientists and scholars in 1862.

But with few people ready to trust him, Flint Jack now found it hard to earn a living. Always a spendthrift, he wasted what little money he had on drink. At Bedford in 1867 he was imprisoned for a year for theft, and after that little is heard of him. Some people believe he died a pauper—a sad end for a man skilled and knowledgeable enough to hoax some of the best brains in the country.

Stokesley Wiseman

In the bygones column of the *Malton Messenger* of 5 September 1863, the following report appeared:

> John Wrightson, of Sedgefield, Co. Durham, later of Stokesley, famous as a wiseman or witch doctor, having made Cleveland too hot to hold him, came to live in Newbiggin, Malton in 1808. He repeated the process here and in 1818 was sentenced to Northallerton prison . . . He was taken away in a horse-drawn Black Maria and poisoned himself as it went through Hovingham.

Did Wrightson deserve such a fate? Not if Canon J. C. Atkinson, author of *Forty Years in a Moorland Parish* can be believed (see p 113). Of Wrightson he says:

> I never heard him spoken of as a man of mischief or as an evil liver, or extortionate . . . No doubt by some he was spoken of with a kind of involuntary or unconscious awe. The impression I was led on to receive was of a man of a not unkindly nature, with a pungent flavour of rough humour about him, shrewd and observant, with a wonderfully well-devised and well-employed means of information.

Wrightson was not the only 'wiseman' practising in the late eighteenth and early nineteenth centuries, but he is the only one remembered in North Yorkshire. He advertised himself as the 'seventh son of a seventh son', a position traditionally thought to confer exceptional powers. A year or two ago a public notice came to light which says:

> The seventh son John Wrightson begs leave to acquaint the public that those who are afflicted with any kind of inward disorder, white swellings, scurvy, or any kind of sores, or shortness of breath, may be relieved by sending him their water. (Likewise any cattle that do not thrive.) He can be of service to them.

Most of Wrightson's business was in providing cures for sick animals, but people consulted him on many other matters.

Some asked for help in detecting thieves or recovering stolen property. Others wanted advice in love affairs. Young men sought protection from conscription, and young girls arrived to have their fortunes told. A large number of people believed they were victims of an 'evil eye' and looked to Wrightson for removal of the curse.

Canon Atkinson believed that Wrightson had a sound knowledge of herbs and drugs, which he used to good effect against routine disorders. But it was Wrightson's supposed powers of black magic that brought him renown. The canon tells of an instance when a coal miner from Fryup consulted Wrightson about the theft of a shirt earlier that day at the pit. Wrightson said the shirt would be at the miner's home when he returned—and sure enough it was. On another occasion, a farm worker from Danby Lodge, now the National Park Centre, called to see Wrightson. Although the two had never met, as soon as the farm worker entered the room, Wrightson said to him: 'Well John, thou's come to ask me about Tommy Frank's black beast'—and he went on to describe the symptoms of the animal's sickness, and its position in the stall.

Canon Atkinson heard this tale from the farm worker himself. In his book the canon speculates that Wrightson probably retained a small but trusted band of informers, including the ostler at an inn. He also suggests that local respect for the wiseman was so high that many thieves would probably rush to return stolen property if they heard he had been consulted.

Wrightson certainly knew how to put on an impressive performance. He wore a long robe and a wizard's pointed hat, complete with mystic symbols. Alongside his crystal ball he had several leather-bound volumes. One of these, the 1753 edition of a book first published in 1555, came into the possession of the late Major J. Fairfax-Blakeborough, of Westerdale. Written by Henry Cornelius Agrippa, it is entitled *The Fourth Book of Occult Philosophy and Geomancy, the Nature of Spirit and Arbate of Magic*—in other words, black magic.

A standard test suggested by Wrightson to discover whether evil was present began with a householder placing a cloth over nine sprigs of elder on a plate. At midnight the plate was to be put near a window. If the sprigs were found scattered the next morning, the devil was active and further help was needed—from Wrightson of course! The wiseman gave firm instructions that no one was to go near the plate until daybreak, and it is impossible not to wonder if he, or one of his assistants, entered the house to disturb the sprigs.

One of the last places where a Wrightson remedy is known to have been applied is Bleach Mill Farm, Kildale. To banish a devil said to be causing sickness and death among the herd of cows, Wrightson prescribed that the heart of one of the dead beasts should be removed. Into the heart were to be inserted nine new needles, nine new pins, and nine new nails. At midnight a fire of rowan had to be brought to its greatest heat, and a psalm was read as the pierced heart was cast into the flames.

Whether the sick animals recovered after this grisly ceremony is not known. But although Wrightson is said to have made a comfortable living for many years, his flight across the moors to Malton, and his subsequent suicide, suggest that his black magic did not always have the desired effect.

Sir George Cayley

A tiny dale on the southern border of the North York Moors has an important place in history. It was the scene of the world's first aeroplane flight. Some people are still amazed by this claim, but the event is beyond dispute. Across the shelving meadowland of Brompton Dale, near Scarborough, Sir George Cayley in 1853 launched a machine that embodied all the basic features of what was to become the aeroplane. Only the lack of a suitable engine, for which Sir George could hardly be held responsible, prevented the Yorkshireman beating the Wright Brothers by a clear fifty years to the first powered flight.

Until a few years ago Sir George was Yorkshire's most neglected hero Even now, after he has received a measure of attention from press and television, he is still inadequately recognised. Alongside the main road at Brompton can be seen the octagonal building in which he worked on the world's first aeroplanes. Its windows are boarded up and there is nothing to indicate its huge significance.

Cayley did not confine himself to aeroplanes. In 1825 he invented caterpillar traction, the basis of all tracked vehicles today. Earlier, when Napoleon was menacing Britain, he produced finned missiles, very like the shells of today. If these had been used instead of being ignored they might have saved Nelson at Trafalgar, for they could out-shoot any cannon. Cayley also did much work on railway safety; he designed the first machine for testing streamlined shapes; he suggested the use of sloping floors for theatres; and it is to him, and his aeroplanes, that we owe the bicycle wheel.

Born at Scarborough on 27 December 1773, Cayley succeeded to the Brompton baronetcy in 1792. It was only seven years later, still in the eighteenth century, that he ushered in the notion of the aeroplane.

Until then, efforts at flight, except by balloon, had been based on imitating the flapping wings of a bird. Cayley preferred the image of a bird with its wings kept still, as if gliding. This fixed-wing concept is shown on a silver disc produced by Cayley and now in the care of the Kensington Science Museum. The design is regarded as the first picture of an aeroplane.

The vision that inspired Cayley is revealed by these words written by him in 1816: 'An uninterrupted navigable ocean that comes to the threshold of everyman's door ought not be neglected as a source of human gratification.' Cayley did not neglect it. In 1804, by fixing a kite face downwards across a pole, with a movable cross-shaped tail, he constructed a model glider. He wrote: 'It was very pretty to see it sail down a steep hill, and it gave the idea that a larger instrument would be a better and safer conveyance down the Alps than even the sure-footed mule.' Technically, this glider is the world's first aeroplane, although it did not offer flight to man. Cayley particularly observed: 'The least inclination of the tail made it shape its course like a ship by a rudder.'

There is little doubt that Brompton Dale was the setting for this experiment. Later flights certainly took place there. In 1809 Cayley built a large, 300sq ft glider. Again he sailed it from hill to plain, noting: 'When any person ran forward in it . . . it would bear upward so strongly as scarcely to allow him to touch the ground.' This is the first known flight by a full-size scientifically designed aeroplane.

Cayley had already used a 'whirling arm', or propeller, as an aid to flight. Unfortunately, he abandoned this idea, probably because of the all-important absence of an engine. But in 1818 Cayley designed the first wheeled undercarriage. The particular problem was to combine lightness with strength, and this led Cayley to produce the tension wheel, later adopted by the bicycle. Meanwhile, in three historic papers written in 1809–10, Cayley set out for the first time the modern theory of aerodynamics: he was the first person to observe such important principles as the superior uplift given by a cambered wing to a flat one.

In 1852 Cayley published a glider design showing every basic feature of the modern aeroplane except wing flaps. More important, in 1849 and 1853 he built tri-plane gliders largely conforming to this design. Besides fixed main wings they had an adjustable tailplane-cum-fin, a pilot-operated elevator-cum-rudder, and a light three-wheel undercarriage. Of the 1849 machine, which he later described as 'the old flyer', Cayley reported that a 'boy of about ten was floated off the ground for several yards on a descending hill'.

The 1853 flight was more spectacular and is now regarded as the first man-carrying flight by a heavier-than-air machine— the true birth of the aeroplane. Brompton Dale was again the scene. Cayley's coachman was selected for the flight, and Cayley's granddaughter, then a young girl, left this account:

Everyone went out on to the high east side and saw the start from close to. The coachman went into the machine and landed on the west side at about the same level. The coachman got out and when the watchers had got across, he shouted: 'Please Sir George, I wish to give notice. I was hired to drive, not fly.' The machine was put away in a barn, and I used to hide in it.

38

The distance covered by the flight was about 140ft. Although flying did not become practical until the Wright brothers' flight of 1903, it is worth re-emphasising that the machine the brothers flew was an advance on Cayley's only in the addition of an engine. And Cayley happens to be the first man who suggested that an internal combustion engine could be used to power an aeroplane!

What the local people thought of Cayley is perhaps indicated by his comment that, to the public, 'aerial navigation is a subject rather bordering on the ludicrous'. His farmer-neighbours were probably more impressed by a drainage scheme he devised, which remains his most lasting monument in the moors. To prevent flooding around Malton, he suggested cutting an overflow channel for the Derwent. Controlled by a lock and now known as the Scalby Cut, this channel follows the pre-Ice Age course of the Derwent, reaching the coast at Scalby, near Scarborough.

Cayley died at Brompton Hall in 1857. On the centenary of his death, a cherry tree was planted in the grounds of the hall, today a county council special school. A portrait of Cayley hangs in the National Portrait Gallery, and both his London house and his Scarborough birthplace (in a street named Paradise) are marked by plaques. All this is still relatively small beer, and it has been suggested that a statue or obelisk should be erected, perhaps in Brompton Dale. The many-sided Sir George seems to deserve no less.

The Hermit of Rosedale

For a quarter of a century George Baxter was the Hermit of Rosedale. To give him the titles he preferred he was also Lord Rosedale, the Sultan of Zanzibar, and the Admiral of the French Fleet.

Baxter used these forms of address scornfully in long and bitter battles against authority. His hostility was directed in particular at his local district council—and if the Admiral of the Fleet was a little short of cannon power, he had a well-oiled shotgun, which he seldom hesitated to use.

Baxter lived for more than forty years at Woodlands Farm, Thorgill, Rosedale. He was a member of a West Riding family, and for several years after he arrived in the district he took a normal part in local life. But gradually he withdrew from almost all social contact. From 1934 until his death in 1959 his seclusion was virtually complete. Although he would exchange a few words with neighbours as he walked round his fields, he rarely left his farm and did his best to avoid its few callers. A local woman, Mrs Mabel Blacklock, left his groceries and mail on the doorstep and collected any letters for posting. Baxter even boarded up his windows.

From behind the barricades he conducted his campaigns. He refused to sign documents surrendering grazing rights on the common at Appleton-le-Moors. Eventually, he was the only one of 160 common-right holders not to agree to a move intended to allow the rights on 139 acres of the common to revert to the Manor of Spaunton.

Baxter also refused to pay his rates. Efforts at enforcement culminated in the issuing of a writ against the hermit's property. Although it was the district council's task to serve this writ, no volunteer could be found in Kirbymoorside or Pickering. Eventually, a London inquiry agent accepted the job. He set out fearlessly enough but retreated to a warning blast from the hermit's gun—a response most local people had anticipated. Even a policeman, who approached the cottage disguised as a grocery delivery man, had to face the menacing double barrels. Ironically, the officer's name was Tom Shooter!

The reason, or reasons, for Baxter's self-imposed exile are unknown, although there is the inevitable talk of unrequited love. Baxter almost certainly suffered agonising loneliness at Woodlands Farm for, after his death, it was discovered that he had made companions of rats. Loaves of bread were hung in various places for the rodents, and Baxter had even made runs for them between different rooms.

On 10 March 1959, few mourners were present when Baxter's body was lowered into grave No. 1926 in Pickering Churchyard. But while Baxter had rejected the world, the world had not entirely turned its back on him. The will of a brother, Charles, who died in 1960, contained a request that George's body be re-interred in the family grave in Nab Wood Cemetery, Shipley. Late in 1972 this request was quietly carried out—perhaps the best possible conclusion to a sad story.

Frank Elgee

In the summer of 1898 a seventeen year old boy viewed the countryside from a wheelchair by a stream at Ingleby Greenhow. Years later he wrote:

> My mother used to wheel me down, and even then I would sit for hours watching the birds—wagtails, dippers, redstarts, and swallows. I also used to sit in a garden facing the Cleveland Hills, watching the rosy light of the sun flash on their craggy summits, or observing the insects on the flowers.

This was probably the beginning of a remarkable bond that gives Frank Elgee the pre-eminent right to be named the 'man of the moors'.

A memorial to Elgee, a flat-topped moorland boulder, stands near Ralph Cross on Blakey Ridge. Besides giving Elgee's name and the dates of his birth and death—1880 and 1944—the inscription contains only two words: 'Naturalist. Archaeologist.' Although the simplicity is admirable, neither the inscription nor the job held by Elgee at the peak of his career—curator of the Dorman Museum, Middlesbrough—gives much indication of his special relationship with the moors or his vast contribution to their appreciation.

The son of a pay-clerk at a Middlesbrough ironworks, Elgee left school at fourteen. He worked for a short time in an office, but a severe attack of pneumonia soon put him into hospital and afterwards the wheelchair. His parents sent him to recover at Ingleby Greenhow, where the family had spent several happy summer holidays. Elgee's debt to that time is clear from the recollections in his diary.

Although Elgee was quickly free of the wheelchair, his lifelong poor hearing and sight are still blamed on that early illness. Despite his limited formal education, he became

41

assistant curator at the Dorman Museum in 1904. He was by that time deeply interested in the moors, and eight years later his knowledge emerged in his first book, *The Moorlands of North-East Yorkshire*. In 1930 this was supplemented by *Early Man in North-East Yorkshire*, after which he and his wife, Harriet, wrote *The Archaeology of Yorkshire*, published in 1933.

All these books remain regional classics even though they now need to be read against later research. Probably the most valuable for the general reader is *Moorlands*, a largely topographical work. But Elgee also set down his experiences of the moors in his diary. Here perhaps is where Elgee's unique affinity with the moors is most strikingly revealed. No one has responded more intimately to the moorland landscape or communicated its qualities with greater feeling and force.

In his description of a walk from Hutton Gate, Guisborough, in September 1917, Elgee captures the essence of moorland beauty—the subtle effects of light and shade on the horizon:

> You have been urged upwards by that love for summits which is the mountaineer's joy. Suddenly you overtop the last rise, to behold a vast expanse of elevated moorland . . . This moorland resembles nothing so much as a heaving sea, wave behind wave, swell merging into swell, hollow into hollow. Every moment you expect the crests to break into foam. Instead, shafts of silvery sunlight shoot down from behind the clouds, to reveal the blended greys, greens and reds of a variegated vegetation. The light withdraws, and once more the moorland becomes sea—a strange immovable sea whose mountain-high waves have ceased to surge forward . . . so that puny man might wonder and admire, generation after generation.

Elgee's feeling for all facets of the moors was intense: he could not get close enough to the landscape. In June 1927 he records following a paved way near Cock Heads, Glaisdale:

> The footsteps of the generations have worn deep hollows in the stones. Reverently I add mine to those of pannierman, farmer, forester, man-at-arms, esquire, knight, baron, the medieval ironworkers, and all the motley throng, less enduring than the stones on which they rudely tramp.

Recounting a walk by Black Beck, near Castleton on 12 May

1912, when he was thirty-two, Elgee says: 'I took off my boots and stockings and walked barefoot on the turf and the bog moss and the crowberry, finally paddling in the stream.' And describing a view of Scugdale, he declares: 'I look into uncharted land, I am the first to set eyes on the scene, I am back before man beheld it.'

In Elgee's diary, we find him noting details such as the 'most graceful undulatory motion' of a slow-worm moving through bracken. At Fen Bog on 22 August 1912, he saw two adders:

> I pointed one out to a gentleman, a lay-reader, a Sunday school teacher, a teetotaller, non-smoker, an instructor of the young, and to my amazement he most ferociously attacked the inoffensive reptile, battering it on the head with his stick until it was lifeless.

Elgee's wife, a Northallerton schoolteacher, first met her future husband when he was throwing a boomerang on Danby Moor! She is said to have sometimes walked naked around their home at Commondale, where Elgee himself, in defiance of his poor health, sometimes slept on the verandah. The house is now named Woodlands.

Elgee's books eventually earned him an honorary PhD from Leeds University. Earlier, in 1923, he had been appointed curator of the Dorman Museum. But after only nine years, a recurrence of pneumonia compelled him to give up the job. The illness also brought a change of home for the Elgees—first to Guisborough and then, in search of a milder climate, to Alton, Hampshire, where Elgee is buried.

Before her death in 1972, Mrs Elgee expressed regret that her husband was not buried in the moors. His Blakey Ridge memorial, unveiled by Mrs Elgee in 1953, was put up by no fewer than ten Yorkshire societies. Positioned opposite the Rosedale Road, it overlooks the scene of Elgee's great archaeological dig on Loose Howe (see p 23). In 1968 the Dorman Museum instituted an annual Frank Elgee Memorial Lecture. There is certainly no danger that Elgee will be forgotten, but it seems a particular pity that his diary has never been published, for it is one of the finest documents ever to come out of the moors.

3

INDUSTRY

Whitby Whalers

The daily scene on Whitby fish quay, with boxes of cod or crab being landed from modest inshore fishing boats, makes it hard to imagine a time when broad-beamed whaling vessels keeled into the port to unload their gargantuan catches. But between 1753 and 1837, 577 whaling voyages were made from Whitby, which was one of Britain's foremost whaling ports.

A leading Whitby skipper, William Scoresby, came to be regarded as the most daring and successful of all whaling men. The son of a farmer at Cropton, near Pickering, he made thirty trips and captured 533 whales—more than any other European whaler. Seeking better means of sighting the whales he invented the crow's nest. The first was introduced in 1807 and consisted of a wooden frame covered with leather and canvas. It included space for a telescope, a compass, signal-flags, a speaking trumpet, and a musket. A movable screen was provided to protect the sailor on look-out.

Scoresby's catches were usually two-and-a-half to four times greater than those of rival skippers. His skill as a navigator, allied to a unique sailing technique, enabled him to reach the whaling grounds before the rest of the fleet. Scoresby put his trust in exceptionally heavy ballast. Once the ship was moving, the ballast tended to impel the vessel forward under her own momentum. It also helped Scoresby's ship to sail more successfully against the wind than any other vessel. Rival skippers, while ready to copy some of Scoresby's other ideas, including modifications to sails and spars, feared that heavy ballast would worsen any collision with the ice. Their timidity meant that on one occasion Scoresby caught fourteen whales before his fellow whalers arrived. In 1806 he had enough time to pursue the whales to within 510 miles of the North Pole, the furthest point ever reached by a sailing ship.

In those days, the capture of the whale was made from small boats, with none of the powerful weapons and sophisticated aids that have made modern whaling such a shameful story. Scoresby himself led these perilous excursions. Over 6ft tall and powerfully built, he was an expert with the harpoon, thrown by hand.

Scoresby's eldest son, also named William, was even more remarkable. He made his first whaling voyage at the age of ten, as a stowaway on his father's ship. There is a story that when he asked his father what his mother would say, his father replied: 'She'll be all the more glad to see you when you get home.' Scoresby Junior became a master whaler at twenty-one, but twelve years later, in 1833, he abandoned the sea to become a priest in the Church of England. After serving at Bessingby, near Bridlington, he moved to Liverpool, where a few years earlier he had landed the largest cargo of blubber ever seen in the port!

Scoresby Junior spent whaling's close season studying at Edinburgh University. Local scorn clearly prompted his comment: 'Let the Whitby people say what they will about the college. I find it is the best thing I ever did . . .' And so it was, for Scoresby became a skilled and respected scientist. While whaling he carried out a detailed study of magnetic fields, with the aim of producing a compass untroubled by magnetism. He also made the first correct map of East Greenland. Even as an apprentice he decorated the ship's logs with drawings showing the detailed composition of snowflakes and the anatomy of whales, and in 1820 his observations blossomed into a book that is still a standard source work: *An Account of the Arctic Regions with a History and Description of the Northern Whale Fishery.*

When Whitby's whaling trade began, two ships were sent out. By 1776 the number had increased to 15, although 8 was more usual. The largest size attained by the fleet was 20 ships, in the 3 successive years 1786–8. Manned by 40–50 men, the ships weighed up to 350 tons and were characterised by square rigged sails and broad heavy bows for ramming a passage through the ice. Their special 'whaling' arrangements included the 'flensing platform', a broad deck of wood lowered over the bulwarks to allow the fishermen to cut up the whale while it was still in the sea. This, too, was an invention of the elder Scoresby.

The ships sailed from Whitby in February–March and returned between June and September. For many years a voyage was thought successful if it produced 4 or 5 whales. But between 1790 and 1823 the average per ship was 15.

The largest single catch was not by either of the Scoresbys but by another fine whaling skipper, Captain Kearsley, who landed 28 whales from the *Resolution* in 1814. This haul yielded 230 tons of oil, closely matching the overall average of 8 tons per whale. Altogether 1814 was the peak year of Whitby whaling, with 8 ships bringing home 172 whales. The blubber, boiled in 4 harbourside oil houses, produced 1,730 tons of oil, which was sold for oil lamps. The carcases yielded 42 tons of whalebone fins, which became 'stays' in the corsetry trade.

By this time whaling was the lifeblood of Whitby. Each successful voyage was worth about £3,000 to the town. Scoresby Senior is said to have earned £2,000 a year—perhaps £70,000 by today's standards!

But a serious decline was about to set in. The spread of gas lighting reduced the demand for oil, and changes in fashion for a time made 'stays' virtually redundant. Catches were in any event becoming too small to be economic, and the fleet also suffered a disastrous series of shipwrecks. Scoresby Senior retired in 1823, aged sixty-three, after his ship was burned out in The Orkneys. Three years later Whitby experienced its worst ever whaling season up to that time. Of 5 ships sent out, 2 were wrecked, with the loss of all but 3 lives, and the others returned with poor catches.

By 1831 only one ship, the *Phoenix*, was engaged in whaling. On her 1832 trip she landed the largest cargo of oil—234 tons— ever brought into Whitby. This encouraged a second vessel, the *Camden*, to try her luck, and for a short period the two ships returned some good catches. But in 1837 the *Phoenix*, setting out on her twenty-second voyage, was wrecked off the harbour mouth. The *Camden's* voyage in the same year was a failure, and after eighty-four years the whaling trade was abandoned. In the boom era, from 1766 to 1816, 2,761 whales had been landed in the port.

Whitby's most prominent reminder of the enterprise is a handsome whalebone arch on the West Cliff, each year framing thousands of tourist photographs. The arch was obtained in 1963 by Mr Graham Leach of Sandsend, who organised a competition among Norwegian whalers, the prize being the honour of having the whalebones erected in Whitby. The arch is formed by the jawbones of a whale 82ft long and weighing 111 tons, captured in the Weddell Sea.

Many original links with whaling still exist. Scoresby Senior's birthplace is a cottage called Nutholme, near Cropton. His two Whitby homes also survive—the red-brick Scoresby House in Church St, and No 13, Bagdale, where he died in 1829, aged sixty-nine. Exhibited in Whitby Museum is a pump he erected in Church Street with a Latin inscription saying: 'Water for the free use of all. Draw and drink but don't gossip.' The museum also contains the younger Scoresby's scientific papers and instruments, including the compound magnetic needle that he invented as the solution to the compass problem. At the age of sixty-six Scoresby sailed to Australia specially to test this instrument. By this time he had become a Doctor of Divinity and Master of Arts and had been elected a Fellow of the Royal Society. On a visit to the USA he was well enough known to be received by President John Tyler at the White House: the ever observant Scoresby noticed that there were signs of heavy spitting on the marble portico!

When Scoresby Junior left the sea he made a notable mark as a social reformer. At Bradford, where he served before retiring to Torquay, he fought hard for better sanitation and a reduction in air pollution. He also founded schools and helped to start a 'Friendly Society', which ran its own bank and provided sickness benefits for factory girls. His last visit to Whitby was to deliver a lecture on magnetic variation. It is nice to think that a few of his listeners reflected on the unlikely homecoming of a former child stowaway on a whaler.

Ironstone

In 1964 a director of Dorman Long, the iron and steel company, uttered some memorable words: 'It is finished irrevocably now.' He was referring to Cleveland ironstone. The closure of Skelton pit between Saltburn and Whitby brought to an end one of the longest—and ultimately the most spectacular—chapters in the industrial history of the North York Moors.

The story spans 2,000 years. Until not long ago it could be traced over only half that period, but in the early 1960s there was great excitement when a complete Iron Age smelting furnace, or bloomery, was discovered on Levisham Moor. The reason for the excitement was that very few bloomeries of the Iron Age, which immediately preceded the arrival of the Romans, have been found in Britain. Dated 550BC, the simple clay-lined furnace at Levisham gives the North York Moors a link with the earliest iron-making in Britain, beginning about 800BC.

But although the Levisham furnace is 1,000 years older than any other known to exist in the moors, bloomeries using essentially the same methods were established in large numbers during the medieval period. The sites of 120 have been identified and there were probably many more. Each furnace could produce only between $1\frac{3}{4}$ and $2\frac{1}{2}$ tons of iron a year, and they had relatively short lives governed by the availability of ore and

Plate 1 The spirit of the moors — a classic vista across the head of Rosedale. The view contains many elements of the moorland scene: a rolling road, grazing sheep, the rough moor giving way to the gentler dale, and a wide but high horizon

Plates 2 and 3 Attitudes to landscape: *(above)* unashamedly practical, the Roman Road strikes boldly across the moors towards the coast. Beauty has arisen out of need; *(below)* the Rievaulx Terrace. Created solely for pleasure it is one of England's most subtle and satisfying examples of landscaping

fuel. In 1963 an excellent example was excavated on the hillside above Bransdale House Farm, Glaisdale. Sunk into the ground, it is an oval stone-lined hollow about 8ft long and 3ft wide, with a flue rising to ground level and a mass of slag embedded in the base.

The usual method of obtaining ore for the bloomeries was simply to dig down to the seam and chip out as much ore as possible. From the shape of these holes, which broaden out at the bottom where the seam was attacked, they are now known as the Bell Pits. They vary in depth from about 7ft to 20ft and are usually found in clusters. About 175 of the pits are on a heather-and-bracken covered moor at Goathland, and there is a further very large group, some sprouting trees, at Delves near Egton Bridge. Until early this century they were regarded as dwellings of the ancient Britons.

The era of the small bloomery effectively ended in 1577 when what was probably the first blast-furnace in the North of England was built in the North York Moors—near Rievaulx Abbey! The exact site of this surprising development has never been located, but the Rievaulx furnace, and its successor built in the same area in 1616, produced 100–280 tons of iron annually for seventy years. Sone of the iron was used in a nearby forge but much was stored at York and sold on the open market. Iron-making at Rievaulx probably ceased when a ban on the use of wood as a fuel for furnaces was imposed in the middle of the seventeenth century. This hastened the movement of the iron industry to areas with ready access to coal.

For 200 years the moorland ironstone lay dormant, its wildest fling yet to come. This arrived when it fired the northern skies in the Industrial Revolution.

Beginning in 1801, the Tyne Iron Company used ironstone nodules gathered on the beaches between Saltburn and Scarborough. But local attempts at that time to exploit the rich inland deposits met with failure: sample after sample was greeted with derision or indifference by leading iron companies.

A breakthrough came in 1837 when the Birtley Iron Company, Co Durham, accepted delivery of a second trial cargo of ironstone, from a seam discovered at Grosmont during the building of the Whitby–Pickering Railway. Pleased with the ore, the Birtley company contracted for more, and soon other companies followed suit. In 1842 and 1844 two blast-furnaces were built on Tyneside specially for the Grosmont ore, which was by then being delivered to every major ironworks in the North East.

With coal available via the new railways, ironworks soon sprang up in the moors themselves. Between 1858 and 1860 two blast-furnaces and 33 cottages (all now demolished) were built at Beck Hole. The enterprise employed 180 men but was wound up in 1864. Not far away, the double row of cottages that today forms the hamlet of Esk Valley were associated not with this venture but with a little-known ironstone mine, worked intermittently for about seventeen years until 1877.

A plan to build a blast-furnace at Esk Valley never materialised, but reasonable success attended ironworks at Grosmont, where two furnaces were in blast in 1863; a third was added in 1875, and production continued until 1891. The family named Clark, who owned the mining rights, built the Victorian house, The Hollins. Mrs Clark was the daughter of the whaling skipper, William Scoresby Senior, (see p 44). A feature of The Hollins was a passage from a lounge to the mine, giving easy access for the ironmaster.

The home of another ironmaster, the Grange, Glaisdale, still includes an unusually low window, inserted to enable the ironmaster to scan his works—and his workmen—through binoculars! These works were in operation between 1866 and 1876. Tubs conveyed the ore downhill through a tunnel from the moorland seam. The tubs emerged from the tunnel to cross the Esk by a viaduct, an abutment of which still stands. The works included three furnaces and two chimneys, one 252ft high. For a time the Angler's Rest became the Three Blastfurnaces.

Meanwhile a combined cement works and ironworks arose at the north end of Runswick Bay. The principal features were two furnaces, an engine house, and a chimney. Cranes lifted coal from ships berthed in a harbour cut from the rock.

The sea has claimed this venture, but within two miles to the north, the crumbling harbour of Port Mulgrave remains as a striking monument to the nineteenth-century iron age. Built in the 1850s for the shippage of ironstone to Sir Charles Palmer's works at Jarrow, the harbour once handled 3,000 tons of ore per week. Shafts were sunk from the clifftop to the seams, and the ore was discharged at the quay through a tunnel, now blocked up. At first, sailing ships transported the ore, but these were soon replaced by barges, towed by paddle steamers. Eventually, the harbour was linked by a 3-mile narrow-gauge railway to workings at Grinkle Park, where Sir Charles Palmer built the country house that is now an hotel. Worth seeking among the rhododendrons are the nineteen tiny headstones marking the graveyard of the Palmer dogs. This is one of three canine cemeteries within the moors, the others being at Arden Hall, Hawnby, and (an interesting recent addition) by the roadside in Pockley.

The greatest ironstone Klondyke in the moors was undoubtedly Rosedale (see also p 125). In 1851 the population of the valley was 558. Twenty years later it was 2,839—and perhaps that total could be doubled if lodging miners are added. Yorkshire contributed under half the miners and, contrary to popular assumption, there were very few Irish immigrants. But there was a large influx from depressed Norfolk and Lincolnshire, and experienced miners even arrived from the Cornish clay and tin mines, in response to a special recruiting campaign.

To obtain stone for their homes and the mines, the workmen plundered the ruins of Rosedale Abbey, leaving only the fragment seen today. Some of the stone went into a lecture hall and schoolroom that still stands: in the frantic years it served as a hospital.

The first Rosedale mine was on the hillside above Hollins Farm, Rosedale West. Between 1856 and 1885 it yielded over 3 million tons of high grade ore. Like most of the Rosedale output this was sent to blast-furnaces in County Durham.

The second mine, Sheriff's Pit, active between 1857 and 1911, is best identified by a fenced-off shaft, 2 miles north of

Rosedale Abbey, near the old railway line. The workings were down the hillside, and a tunnel was driven from them to the foot of the 270ft shaft, up which the ore was raised to the surface. Thirty-two ponies worked at the mine, and their former loading bay can be seen by the entrance to the tunnel, among tips above Medds Farm.

The most successful mines were those of Rosedale East, which worked with only slight breaks from 1865 until all mining ceased in 1926. Up to 100 men were employed on each shift. From Stable Farm the track taken by ponies to various drifts can still be picked out.

Life in Rosedale during the boom years had a true frontier flavour. As one miner tumbled out of bed to report for his shift, another clambered in. One man, John Barthram, lived in a railway cabin, in which his wife gave birth to their baby. John, a tub-tipper, was lame, and he crossed railway lines by pulling his disabled leg with a rope.

The miners created their own entertainment. One earned 5s (25p) per night playing at hunt balls on a violin made from animal gut and pit roofing timber. There were pigeon shoots, challenge horse races, and the annual Abbey Sweepstakes. A Kirbymoorside jeweller frequently walked to Rosedale with a caseful of watches on Friday night, selling every one before returning home on Sunday.

As late as 1931 the population of Rosedale was still almost 1,000, but by 1961 it had fallen to 291—less than in pre-mining days . . . Rosedale's tumultuous interval was little more than a memory.

Alum

On 17 December 1829, heavy rain caused a dramatic collapse of the cliffs between Sandsend and Runswick Bay, sending the entire hamlet of Kettleness sliding into the sea. Fortunately, the inhabitants had taken shelter in a ship, the *Little Henry*, lying just offshore. The vessel had arrived to collect alum, but this was one cargo she would have to forego, for not only was

Kettleness village destroyed but so were its alum works, which did not resume production for two years.

Alum is still used in tanning, dyeing, papermaking, and the production of drugs. Britain's first alum mine was established at Belman Bank, Guisborough, in the North York Moors, in about 1595. The mine is believed to have been started after Guisborough's squire, Sir Thomas Chaloner, on a trip to Europe, noticed a similarity in colouring between leaves on trees near the Pope's alum works at Rome and those growing back home at Belman Bank. Also common to both districts was a frost-resistant clay, mostly white but with yellow and blue speckles. On clear nights this clay 'sparkled like glass on the road'.

Chaloner is sometimes said to have had a papal curse issued against him for bribing some of the Pope's alum workers to leave Italy and smuggling them to England in casks. Other versions of the Belman Bank enterprise, however, say that Chaloner recruited his first workers honestly, in France.

Immediately before the Guisborough mine opened, Britain was paying the Pope £52 per ton for alum. The enormous savings introduced by the mine can be judged by the price of only £11 per ton for Britain's home-produced alum more than 200 years later. The Belman Bank mine itself was exhausted within twenty-five years and two other Guisborough workings were also short-lived. But new alum mines, usually accompanied by processing works, appeared throughout the northern half of the moors, from Old Peak near Robin Hood's Bay in the east to Thimbleby in the west.

Built in about 1728, the Kettleness works were quite large, but they were greatly overshadowed by works at nearby Sandsend, where production began in 1615. The bare headland of Sandsend Ness owes its outline and its lack of vegetation to the vast quantities of alum waste piled there. The car park at the foot of Lythe Bank stands on the site of the former alum-shipping wharves, and at low tide near the foot of the Ness the bases of wooden mooring posts are revealed, embedded in the rock.

But the two biggest mines in Britain, also established in 1615, were at Boulby and Loftus. By a remarkable coincidence, Britain's first potash mine, where production began in 1973, occupies almost the same site as the Boulby alum mine, described by the Rev John Graves, in his *History of Cleveland* (1808) as being 'on the verge of a stupendous cliff'. To Graves the mine was 'at once pleasing, awful, and magnificent'. He wrote a valuable account of the mine in operation, in which the following passage, noting a curious system of 'barrows, half-barrows and quarter-barrows', is particularly interesting:

> As the alum rock lies at a considerable depth below the surface of the ground, the labour of removing it is attended with much labour and expense. But this part of the business is conducted with such order and regularity, as not only to equalise the labour to the strength of the different workmen but also to enforce it in proportion to their wages. For this purpose they have wheelbarrows of various sizes, denominated *barrows, half barrows* and *quarter barrows*.
>
> The workmen are divided into two parties, with an *overseer* or *tally-man*, to see that the assigned number of journeys is duly performed; and as they all run the same distance, whilst one party is out upon the journey, the other is employed each in filling his own barrow, which prevents all interruption and confusion. By thus proportioning the size of the barrows to the strength of the workmen, boys of twelve or fourteen years of age find employment; and when a man, through age or infirmities, finds himself unequal to a barrow of the largest size, he has an opportunity of making choice of a smaller, his earnings being always in proportion.

Altogether, the alum industry cannot have contributed much to local charm. The alum 'rock' is really shale, which was treated in a most extraordinary way to produce usable alum. The lengthy and unsavoury process began with the burning or calcining of the shale over a brushwood fire. The burned shale was then steeped in water, which absorbed its qualities to become liquid alum. If this liquid proved too weak it was pumped back over a fresh pile of calcined shale, a process known as 'working the liquor'. Eventually the liquid was run into cisterns where the impurities were allowed to settle. Conveyed by troughs to the 'alum house' it next underwent continuous boiling for twenty-four hours. Boulby had no fewer than eighty boiling pans—a true hell's cauldron.

But the most disagreeable stages of the process were yet to come. The boiled liquid was run into settling tanks and mixed with a solution prepared from burned seaweed—kelp—and human urine. The purpose was to reduce the specific gravity to the point at which the liquid would crystallise. Since 20 tons of seaweed were needed to make 1 ton of kelp, the collecting and burning of seaweed became a major industry in its own right. The seaweed had to be continuously stirred and raked as it burned. Large quantities of urine were shipped from London and some was collected in towns and villages near the alum works. There are records of human urine being bought at Great Ayton and Guisborough for one old penny per gallon.

In 1794 both kelp and urine began to be replaced by 'black ashes', obtained by burning the dregs from soap-making boilers; but within ten years there was a more sophisticated change when control of the specific gravity was achieved by an additive based on muriate of potash.

After being allowed to settle yet again, the mixture was run into a fresh set of pans, where it was stirred, or 'roused', before being left for about four days. During this time primary crystallisation took place—but the crystals were immediately dissolved by being boiled in a pan containing just enough water to cover them. This produced a highly concentrated liquid alum, which was poured into casks. During the next fortnight a second and final crystallisation occurred, with the alum clinging to the sides of the casks. When scraped off it was ready to be packed in barrels and sold. Altogether about 120–130 tons of calcined shale were needed to produce 1 ton of alum.

In the early seventeenth century 800 men were employed in this trade around Whitby. A side product was rough salt, known as 'rough Epsoms'. This was sold for £3 per ton. Alum shale could also be converted into a form of whitewash, and the licensee of the former Bence Bridge Inn, Stokesley (today a smallholding) doubled his duties as a publican by travelling the district selling this mixture.

The location of most of the major works, on the coast but generally with no safe anchorage nearby, created a need for ships that could beach themselves safely and be loaded at low tide. Vessels like the *Little Henry* were built to meet this need. Broad beamed but flat bottomed, they appear in many prints of old Whitby, apparently stranded on the rocks. They could carry 30–60 tons and were worked by only three or four men. The building of these ships was another local industry. Most of their trade was with London, but they sometimes took alum abroad.

Since the alum shales are among the oldest rocks in the national park, the history of alum is punctuated by the discovery of prehistoric fossils, some of immense size. A huge plesiosaur, found at Loftus, fills a wall in the Yorkshire Museum, York. Several similar fossils are on view in Whitby Museum, including an ichthyosaurus, also uncovered at Loftus, and a teleosaurus, or giant crocodile, dug from the alum shale at Saltwick, south of Whitby. A harbour was constructed here for alum a year after mining started in 1649, and a huge blockstone, upturned by the sea but still with the date 1766 visible in letters 1ft high, indicates the building of a new quay. The works closed in 1791, and 102 years later a start was made on laying-out part of the nearby cliffs as a tea garden. Beneath the foundation stone of the tea house was placed a sealed bottle containing coins and a copy of the *Whitby Gazette*. The area is still known locally as The Tea Gardens.

Other notable works in the Whitby district were at Low Peak and Stoupe Brow, Ravenscar. Opened in 1640 they jointly produced 300 tons of alum in 1816, with 8 boiling pans and 65 workmen. They closed in 1862, but there, too, low tide reveals mooring-post holes, plus a shallow dock cut from the rock.

Inland there is—or rather was—interesting evidence of alum-working at Grosmont. An area of land near the parish church has long been known as the alum garth, and it once contained a building that bore unmistakable signs of having been an alum house. Even at the beginning of the nineteenth century, however, this building was in an advanced state of decay—and the huge size of trees in the immediate vicinity appeared to confirm that work had ceased many centuries before. It could be that the alum house processed shale dug from the nearby river Esk in the monastic period, in defiance of the monopoly then held by the Pope. But the modest scale of the venture, coupled with the long interval that elapsed before a true 'alum industry' was founded allows Belman Bank to retain its claim as Britain's first mine.

The biggest inland mine, however, was at Carlton Bank near Stokesley, active from 1680 to 1809. Like Sandsend Ness the bank displays vast, bare alum tips. The name of the local stream, Alum Beck, also testifies to the considerable former impact of the venture. Yet today many people picnic nearby, enjoying the fine views and totally unaware that a very unpleasant industry once dominated the scene.

Annual production at Carlton averaged about 250 tons, broadly half that of the very biggest works. Production throughout the Moors touched a peak of 5,000 tons in the 1760s, but there was a constant cycle of over-production and under-production, with various works closing and reopening as the price see-sawed. The trade finally collapsed when alum shale was found alongside many coal measures: with fuel to hand it became easier to work the alum near the new coal mines. The last works to close were those at Sandsend in 1867. Their life of 252 years is easily the longest of any single industrial enterprise in the moors and must come close to being a record for the British Isles.

Rievaulx Canals

Among the thousands of people who visit Rievaulx Abbey each year, scarcely one bothers to look at Rievaulx's system of canals. But no study of the abbey is complete without at least a glance at the canals, which are believed to have played a vital part in the creation of the great monastery.

There are two canals, one north of the abbey and one south.

Until a few years ago they were regarded as the former bed of the River Rye, which the monks were thought to have diverted to increase the building area. This theory is still contained in the official guide to the abbey. But the discovery of part of a stone weir near one end of the northern canal was important evidence that the waterways were man-made.

Since the abbey was abundantly served by springs, able to supply drinking water and drive mills, the most likely reason for making the canals was to provide transport. It now seems probable that the monks, or more properly their lay helpers, despatched stone in shallow barges along the new waterways, to be used in the construction of the abbey. If so, this is the earliest known use of a canal in England for an industrial purpose—anticipating the great canal schemes of the eighteenth and nineteenth centuries by up to 700 years.

The industrial role of the canals is virtually proved by the presence in Hollins Wood of an incline or slipway, running between a quarry and the river. The entrance to the southern canal is only a short distance away, and it seems likely that blocks of stone were lowered down the incline and ferried along the canal.

The road from Rievaulx to Helmsley crosses the dried-up bed of this canal, about half a mile from the abbey, near a cottage on the right-hand side. There is no public path here nor at the Hollins Wood incline, but the northern canal forms part of a right of way. Although it can be reached through a gate almost opposite Rievaulx Church, a better plan is to visit the canal as the final section of a short circular walk from the abbey. The first half-mile lies along the Scawton road, but immediately behind Ashberry Farm a track slants back towards the abbey, across the slope of Ashberry Hill. When the trees are not in leaf very attractive views of the abbey are obtained.

The path emerges near a stone bridge designed by John Carr, York's famous Georgian architect. His major works are Harewood House, the Crescent at Buxton, and what is now the Castle Museum, York. But bridges were his bread and butter. The best known and most beautiful is Greta Bridge, formerly in the North Riding but lately transferred to County Durham. In the North York Moors he designed Ingleby Arncliffe hall and the bridges at Hawnby and East Beck, Sandsend; and he widened Ellerbeck bridge by Fylingdales Early Warning Station.

On the Rievaulx side of Carr's bridge, a stile gives access to a path by the river. Halfway along, the point at which the canal diverged from the river can be seen. It was here that the remains of the weir were found. The canal itself, 8ft wide and ¼ mile long, can now be followed its full length, again with excellent views of the abbey. In parts the bed is reedy, and it is not uncommon to find sections filled with water.

With the help of the late John Weatherill, a stonemason at the abbey, members of the Helmsley group of the Yorkshire Archaeological Society some years ago identified various quarries from which stone for the abbey was cut. Linking this research with the dates when different parts of the abbey were built, the group was able to say that if the purpose of the canals was indeed to facilitate the building of the abbey, the northern canal would be in use between 1132 and 1145 and the southern in about 1170. This is a fascinating and valuable piece of detective work that deserves to be much better known.

Jet

Whitby Jet—the words proclaim one of the most famous associations of Yorkshire. And yet, contrary to what even many Yorkshire folk believe, jet is by no means the exclusive preserve of Whitby. Its story, like those of alum and ironstone, ranges widely across the North York Moors.

Jet is a fossilised wood, compressed from a succession of coniferous forests that lived and died about 180 million years ago. It retains the feel of wood but is exceptionally hard. The presence of jet, outcropping near sea level, has influenced the development of much of the bay-and-headland scenery around Whitby. The nabs stand firm on their plinths of jet while the surrounding boulder clays and shales are worn away. Sandsend Ness, Lingrow Knock (Port Mulgrave), and Saltwick Nab and Black Nab, both south of Whitby, have been formed thus.

Next to farming and fishing, the working of jet is probably the oldest industry in the national park. Elaborate jet neck-laces, sometimes of several strings, have been recovered from prehistoric sites in or near the area. During the Roman period jet was used for both jewellery and everyday items such as buttons and hairpins: it is rare for any Roman settlement not to yield some of these objects.

The marriage of Whitby and jet goes back a long way. Whitby Abbey's registers of 1394 include the payment of 7d (about 3p) for seven jet rings made by Robert Carr, who thus becomes the first known Whitby jet worker. About 200 years later, Michael Drayton, in an epic poem celebrating Britain, wrote:

> The rocks by Mulgrave too, my glories forth to set
> Out of their crannied cliffs can give you perfect jet.

But what chiefly forged the link between Whitby and jet was the jet boom of the nineteenth century. Whitby's role in this is said to have been due to a retired naval officer, Capt Tremlett. The carving and shaping of jet into beads and crosses, by knife, file, and rubbing stone, was a well established local industry when Tremlett approached a jet worker named Matthew Hill and suggested the use of machines. Hill was sceptical, but in about 1800 Tremlett paid him to produce the first machine-made jet articles. By 1832 the town still had only 2 jet work-shops, employing 25 people. But by 1870 the Tremlett revo-lution had taken full root. The town contained more than 200 jet workshops employing 1,500 workers. One Whitby crafts-man held a royal appointment as jet-ornament maker to Queen Victoria. On the east side of Whitby one or two former jet work-shops can still be seen—long buildings with frontages almost entirely of glass, divided into many small panes.

From 1850 to 1875 jet dominated the town. A big annual event was the 'Jets' Holiday', with races on the sands. In September 1872 the *Whitby Gazette* reported:

The races came off on the sands as announced on Wednesday afternoon, when a very large company assembled to witness them. This event may appropriately be called the jet workers' festival, for on the day it comes off more than three parts of the jet workshops are closed and the jet workers off for a holiday.

What is the Jets' holiday is the publican's harvest, and the race day of Wednesday was no exception. It brought as it were into focus all the 'fancy' and 'sporting' fraternity and they behaved themselves neither better nor worse than on previous similar gatherings. Thanks to the excellent police arrangements of Supt Ryder, open lawlessness was kept well in check, and all may be said to have passed off quietly.

It is clear that the jet workers were not universally liked, for the *Gazette* went on:

The 'bettors' and others immediately interested in the races were on a level with the horses on the sands, while their 'betters' and some hundreds of quiet spectators looked down upon them from the tops and sloping sides of our glorious cliff.

The day being fine, the latter from their elevated position above the reach of the noise that seems inseparable from a congregation of sporting gentlemen had certainly the most of what enjoyment there may be in seeing poor horses whipped and goaded a mile over those heavy sands.

But jet workers took great pride in their craft. In March 1872 a piece of jet weighing 9lb was found near Sandsend alum works by navvies cutting the Whitby–Loftus railway. Messrs G. and J. Speedy, jet manufacturers, proudly engraved it with the Whitby coat of arms, a view of Mulgrave Castle, and the words Whitby Jet—apparently a clarion call even then. The piece was displayed in Speedy's window, and it would be nice to know where it is now.

A few jet models of Whitby Abbey exist, and in 1968 a retired jet trader refused an American offer of £50 for his model. One Whitby family treasures what it asserts to be the finest example of jet workmanship—a chess board in which the black squares are pure jet and the whites are jet inset with ammonites.

Mounted in an elaborately carved jet frame, the whole board took four years to make.

Ironically, jet's decline had its roots in the peak years of 1870–2, when cheap Spanish jet was used to supplement local supplies. The poor quality of the imported material hastened the swing of fashion against jet. In 1876, only four years after that joyous 'Jets' Holiday', the trade was described as 'very depressed'. By 1884 the number of workers had dropped to under 300, and soon afterwards jet-working withered to the curio level.

In 1966 a bold attempt was made to revive the trade. A Whitby man commissioned designs from some of Britain's leading jewellery designers. Using modern machine tools, his small but carefully trained team of craftsmen produced some truly magnificent jewellery. Many of the pieces were inlaid with gold or diamonds, which brilliantly offset the jet. The prices were high—as much as £400 for a pendant or necklace. But although an exhibition was held in London and a few items were exported, the venture collapsed after three years. However, there are still one or two jet craftsmen, and a pendant inlaid with silver, made by Mr Roy Jay, was presented to the Duchess of Kent when she opened the North Yorkshire Moors Railway in 1973.

In jet's heyday, top quality jet fetched about £1.05 per lb. With a good find easily worth £1,000, miners often risked life and limb by dangling perilously from ropes to reach seams exposed on the cliffs. But much so-called 'Whitby Jet' was mined many miles from the town—which is why it is surprising that Whitby has come to monopolise public interest in the subject.

Spoil heaps from jet workings can be seen in many moorland valleys. In 1871 there were twenty jet sites in Bilsdale, for each of which the operators paid between £15 and £17 to the Helmsley estate. In Rosedale the sites of jet workings can be seen at Cat Nab, Dale Head, and below School Row. Jet was also worked in Scugdale and Farndale.

At Cringle Moor on the Cleveland escarpment, the scramble for jet led in 1852 to an unusual court case, with Mr James

Emmerson, of Easby Hall, alleging that Lord Feversham had trespassed on his land for jet. Before resolving the issue in Mr Emmerson's favour, the court had part of the hillside marked out with pegs. It also ordered the uncovering of the remains of Kirby-in-Cleveland's old alum mines, which both parties accepted had stood on Mr Emmerson's land and which therefore became crucial in determining the exact boundary between the two estates. Lord Feversham had to pay Mr Emmerson £200. Just over half a century later, from 1909 to 1911, the same moor was the scene of probably the last mining of jet—an unsuccessful speculation by a Kirby-in-Cleveland builder.

The method of mining was to drive levels into the hillside. These are now blocked by falls of shale and appear as a row of slight depressions, best seen in a light covering of snow. Not every level produced jet, for the miners sometimes found that the seam had slipped and was inaccessible.

When the mined material was brought out, two men with very fine rakes recovered almost every fragment of jet. Four more men were usually employed, two pick-axing the seam and two wheeling the spoil. Since the only light inside the tunnel was from candles carried by the two miners, special grooves were cut in the floor, one for the outgoing barrow and the other for the incoming one. Each week a local trader took the output of several mines to Whitby.

A little known aspect of the jet industry was the burning of jet shale, to produce a hard red clinker, suitable for making roads. The clinker was usually mixed with pebbles and stones, and farm tenancy agreements often included a requirement that a certain number of cartloads of stone would be delivered annually to the parish 'waywardens'—the highway surveyors of the day. Shale burning gave off an offensive smell and was licensed by the local authority. In the Stokesley district the job was entrusted to Leonard Bowen, of Whorlton, highly skilled at choosing the best place for his 'firebox', a hole carefully angled to make the best use of the prevailing wind. Brushwood was ignited in the hole and the jet shale piled on top. A single hole might be kept burning for as long as ten months.

In the boom years Bowen would no doubt be well known in the Jet Miners' Inn, Great Broughton, a popular place with workmen from the many nearby mines. Displayed at the bar today is a piece of polished jet, with a poem written in 1954 by a passing tramp. I know of no finer tribute:

> Ah! Black as jet, but long ago
> In dignity and lace,
> The ladies wore around their necks
> A flash of ebon grace.
>
> But Oh! Today Great Broughton mourns,
> Still waves the merry corn,
> The beer flows at Jet Miners' Inn,
> But jet's no longer worn.
>
> Still, fashions change, mayhap someday
> Again the craft will thrive,
> And Yorkshire jet will ring the earth
> Black, Flashing, and Alive!

Plates 4 and 5 At Whitby: *(above)* the ancient East Side, with St Mary's Church and the abbey. The pier thrusting forward is the fictional place at which Count Dracula, in the form of a dog, came ashore after being shipwrecked, later running up the 199 steps; *(below)* a contemporary engraving of the 1861 lifeboat disaster in which all but one of the crew died. Overlooking the scene from the partially developed West Cliff is the Royal Hotel, then newly-built as a key feature in George Hudson's scheme for promoting Whitby through his Whitby-Pickering Railway

Plates 6 and 7 The northern hills: *(above)* Roseberry Topping towers dramatically above Newton-under-Roseberry; *(below)* a train on the Esk Valley line approaches Battersby from Great Ayton. In the background is the fine switchback ridge of the Cleveland escarpment — from the left, Hasty Bank, Cold Moor, Cringle Moor and Carlton Bank

4

A LOOK AT LEGENDS

The Beggar's Bridge

The most romantic story in the North York Moors is of the Beggar's Bridge, Glaisdale. The tale is often told, but perhaps not always with concern for its finer detail, and since there are always people fresh to the legend, in which the setting splendidly matches the events, the old tale amply bears retelling.

The bridge at the heart of the story spans the Esk in a single graceful arch near the village railway station. A stone at the crest of the parapet faintly bears the date 1619 and the letters T.F. Though unnoticed by many visitors these are a perfect introduction to the tale. The letters are the initials of Thomas Ferries who was the Beggar; 1619 was the date he built his bridge.

Ferries—mis-spelt Ferris in many accounts—was the son of a moorland sheep farmer. He met Agnes Richardson, the daughter of a wealthy Glaisdale landowner, at the annual St Hilda's fair in Whitby. The couple fell in love, but Agnes' father, who disapproved of Ferries said he would not allow his daughter to marry a beggar. Already hoping to go to sea, Ferries persuaded Mr Richardson to consent to the match if he returned a rich man. The promise is said to have been made with the comment that a thousand things might happen at sea—but yes, if Ferries became a rich man he could marry Agnes.

Ferries sailed from Whitby in 1586 on a ship destined to join the English fleet that conquered the Spanish Armada. Ferries' conduct in the battle won him the praise of Sir Francis Drake, with whom he afterwards sailed to the West Indies. There, Ferries became rich through piracy—no doubt emulating Drake himself. His return to London in 1592 was in a captured foreign vessel, which he sold to increase his fortune. He then travelled to Glaisdale, where Agnes' father kept his word, enabling the lovers to marry.

What of the bridge? Ferries is said to have built it to fulfil a vow he made when crossing the unbridged Esk to see Agnes. Here there are two versions of the story. One is that Ferries was often drenched attempting to ford the Esk. But according to the other, the critical moment came only on the night before Ferries went to sea. In this version, Ferries normally crossed the river without difficulty, perhaps by stepping stomes. But on the final night, 8 May 1588, when Agnes had put a light in her window as a signal that her father was away and it was safe to meet, the river was in flood. Ferries tried unsuccessfully to swim across and was forced to sail without seeing Agnes.

The end of the story, however, is common to both accounts. As an old poem puts it:

> The rover came back from a far distant land,
> And claimed from the maiden her long-promised hand.
> But he built ere he won her the bridge of his vow,
> And the lovers of Egton pass over it now.

Ferries is certainly no imaginary figure. Some people say he was born at Egton, a neighbouring village of Glaisdale, but Lastingham has a stronger claim since it was supported by gifts of money from Ferries in 1620–1 for re-roofing the church and building a new school. As a boy of fourteen Ferries was apprenticed to a Hull ship-owner, and Egton, closer to the sea than Lastingham, perhaps enters the story as a place in which Ferries stayed with friends or relatives while seeking a ship after completing his indentures.

After their wedding, Ferries and his wife settled in Hull, where Ferries quickly built up substantial interest in shipping. In 1614 he was made sheriff of the city and in 1620 he became lord mayor. He was also chosen three times as warden, or honorary head, of the city's Trinity House, the training centre for sailors. After his death in 1630, aged sixty-two, a memorial was erected to him in Hull's Holy Trinity Church. This chiefly depicts an angel giving water to an injured sailor.

The romance between Tom and Agnes is sometmes questioned because searches in the parish records have failed to produce any trace of their marriage. But since the records are incomplete, this evidence, or rather the lack of it, scarcely undermines the story.

The importance of Glaisdale to Ferries is clearly indicated by two bequests in his will—£6 13s 4d (£6·66) to be given annually to the parish priest, at that time based at Danby, and £2 to be donated each year for the upkeep of the parish church. These sums are still paid today. Perhaps more important is that the bridge was commissioned the year after the death of Ferries' wife in 1618. It seems reasonable to assume that the bridge was a memorial to her, although Ferries rather spoils the effect by remarrying in 1620.

Some years ago Hull's Trinity House presented Glaisdale Church with a silver communion service, inscribed in memory of Ferries. The church also contains a copy of a portrait of Ferries that hangs in Trinity House. It is very possible that a badly weathered portion of the inscribed stone on the Beggar's Bridge once bore the Hull crest.

Whoever built the bridge was an artist and craftsman. Strong as well as handsome, the bridge withstood floods in 1930–1 that twice washed away a railway viaduct a short distance downstream. The valley near there is still thickly wooded, a reminder of the time when, in a dalesman's graphic phrase quoted by Canon Atkinson in *Forty Years in a Moorland Parish*, (see p 113) 'a cat swirrel (squirrel) could gan a't'way doon fra Commondale End ti Beggar's Bridge, wivoot yance tooching t'grund'. A very beautiful short walk, most enjoyable in spring and autumn,

71

leads from the bridge through Arncliffe Woods to the Egton Bridge–Rosedale Road.

But at least one incident in the history of the bridge is not picturesque. Early this century there was a sensational accident when a huckster, or farm trader, was crossing the bridge on his horse-drawn cart. With two horses in harness, an older training a younger, the cart had safely descended the 1 in 3 Limber Hill on the Egton side of the bridge. But as it crossed the bridge, the younger horse was startled, perhaps by a passing train. The horse leapt the parapet and was strangled by its harness. Until cut free it dangled grimly above the river—and, surprisingly, photographs of this distressing scene were once common in Eskdale homes.

The Penny Hedge

Visitors to the North York Moors need to rise early to catch the region's best known custom—the planting of Whitby's Penny Hedge. They perhaps also need to consult a diary, for the ceremony takes place on the eve of the Ascension, which is not a date that springs readily to most minds.

Ascension Eve is thirty-eight days after Easter Sunday and usually about 200 people muster for the Penny Hedge ceremony, even though it does start promptly at 9am. Down into the mud of the upper harbour on the east side of the town go three gum-booted countrymen. One holds a horn while the others carry bundles of hazel stakes and branches. The horn-blower stands by as his companions hammer the stakes into the mud and interweave the branches to form a primitive fence. He then blows his horn and calls, 'Out on ye, out on ye, out on ye.' Cameras click and many questions are asked. But the horn-blower and the hedgers now return to the harbourside. The Penny Hedge has been planted.

All this goes back a long way—perhaps to 1159. Legend has it that on 16 October of that year Ralph de Percy, Lord of Sneaton, William de Bruce, Lord of Ugglebarnby, and a companion named Allatson, a freeholder of Fylingdales went hunting. A boar chased by them ran into a cell, or chapel, occupied by a monastic hermit, at Eskdaleside, near Sleights. Some accounts of the story say that the hunters followed the boar into the cell and slew it by the hermit's altar. Other versions claim that the boar died after entering the cell and the hermit shut the door on the hunters. A row certainly developed. The hunters angrily entered the cell and, as an old description puts it, they 'did most violently and cruelly run at the hermit with their boar staves'.

The hermit died from his wounds, either in his cell shortly after the attack or in the hospital at Whitby Abbey several weeks later. As he was dying he is said to have told Whitby's abbot, named Sedman, that he would forgive the culprits in return for a penance. Lacking the hermit's pardon, the men would have faced execution, and when they were brought before the hermit they heard him explain the penance in these terms:

> That upon Ascension Eve, you, or some of you, shall come to the wood of the Stray Heads, which is in Eskdaleside, the same day at sun-rising; and there shall the abbot's officer blow his horn, to the intent that you may know how to find him; and he shall deliver unto you, William de Bruce, ten stakes, eleven stout yowers and eleven yethers, to be cut by you, or some of you, with a knife of one penny price; and you Ralph de Percy shall take twenty-one of each sort, to be cut in the same manner; and you Allatson, shall take nine of each sort, to be cut as aforesaid, and to be taken on your backs, and carried to the town of Whitby; and to be there before nine of the clock the same day beforementioned.
>
> At the same hour, if it be full sea, your labour and service shall cease; and if low water, each of you shall set your stakes to the brim, and so yether them on each side with your yethers, and so stake on each side with your stout stowers, that they may stand three tides without removing by the force thereof: each of you shall do, make and execute the said service all that very hour every year, except it be full sea at that hour, when this service shall cease. You shall faithfully do this in remembrance that you did most cruelly slay me. The officer of Eskdaleside shall blow 'Out on you, out on you, out on you for this heinous crime.' If you or your successors shall refuse this service, you or yours shall forfeit your lands to the abbot of Whitby or his successors.

This is the essence of the Penny Hedge—the knife was to cost one penny, the service was to be performed at 9am on the Ascension Eve, the hedge had to withstand three tides, and failure to perform the task, or to build a strong enough hedge, was to be met by forfeiture of land.

The legend long ago had irreparable holes knocked in it. In his *History of Whitby* (1770) Lionel Charlton pointed out that there was no Ralph de Percy of Sneaton, no William de Bruce of Ugglebarnby, and no Whitby abbot named Sedman. He also observes that surnames such as Allatson did not appear until about 200 years after the wild-boar affair. And finally, no chapel existed on the site of the hermitage until 1224.

Some people say the hedge might originally have been a fish weir, for Ascension Eve is still not too distant from the start of the salmon-fishing season. But there is a more convincing explanation, hinted at in an alternative name for the Penny Hedge—the Horngarth. Tenants of land owned by the Whitby abbot were expected to keep their garths in good order, and it could be that the annual task of maintaining the fences or hedges of the garths was announced by the blowing of a horn. More especially, the horn might have summoned certain local tenants to attend to the upkeep of a single important garth, perhaps the abbot's personal storeyard. The abbot might also have insisted on having his territory staked out to the low-water mark, which would account for the fence being erected in the harbour.

What of the hermit? It is conceivable that when the upkeep of the garths, or garth, was no longer strictly necessary, the abbot, jealous of his rights, continued to compel his tenants to perform a ritualised version of the service. An interesting parallel exists at Pickering where, until early in the nineteenth century, local people were required to pay for the upkeep of a wooden palisade around the castle although the castle had been a ruin since the seventeenth century and no wooden structure had stood there for 500 years! There is a theory that at Whitby, as the original purpose of the Horngarth became obscure, an enterprising monk sat down to produce a fable to match the ceremony—and came up with the Hermit of Eskdale. The abbot's name Sedman bears a marked resemblance to that of Whitby's poet Caedman, once spelt Cedman.

But today's Penny Hedge ceremony does not exactly match the old penance, if it ever has done. The horn is not sounded in the wood. It is not possible to use a 'penny' knife. And the hornblower omits the reference to 'this heinous crime'. But the hazel stakes are cut from a wood at Eskdaleside near the site of the 1224 chapel. This is now a ruined farm building and can be visited on a public right of way.

Since Whitby now has no abbot, the role of the landowner is taken by the Lord or Lady of the Manor of Fyling, currently Miss M. I. Strickland. It is her bailiff who blows the horn, while the planting is carried out by a member of the family that occupies land near Robin Hood's Bay known to have once had an owner named Allatson. Since 1948 the task has been performed by Mr John Hutton, aided by an assistant. Mr Hutton succeeded his brother, who planted the hedge for eight years, and throughout the preceding fifty-two years the hedge was planted by their father. Thus the Hutton family connection dates back to 1888.

From the Eskdaleside wood Mr Hutton takes nine stakes, four stowers, or struts, and nine yethers, or branches, for intertwining. Needless to say no one has known his hedge, or any other, fail to survive three tides. But an intriguing aspect of the penance is the provision that it shall cease if high water ever prevents the hedge being planted. Within memory this has never happened, although Ascension Eve varies from year to year and the tides from day to day.

Since Ascension Eve is governed by Easter, which in turn is linked to the phases of the moon and therefore the tides, this phenomenon is not in itself surprising. Nevertheless, not everyone carries the knowledge at the front of his mind. Did the hermit, on his death bed, just happen to remember that the harbour mud at Whitby, would never be completely covered at 9am on Ascension Eve? Or did an inventive monk carefully do his homework?

Wade—His Wife and His Causeway

Nowhere among the legends of the North York Moors are fact and fancy more strangely mixed than in the story of Wade—his wife and his causeway. Wade is both an identifiable figure in history and a fabled giant. His wife, Bell, is only imaginary, but the causeway is tangible enough—in reality the longest preserved stretch of Roman road in Britain. Perversely, the real Wade had nothing to do with it!

Wade was a powerful Saxon chief who lived at Mulgrave. He is believed to have slain a brutal Northumbrian king named Ethelred in 794 but to have been defeated about four years later at Whalley, in Lancashire, by Ethelred's next-but-one successor Ardulph. Badly wounded, Wade fled to Mulgrave, where he soon died. A prominent stone in a field near East Barnby crossroads is regarded as marking his grave. Once there were two stones, and the distance between them, about 12ft, was said to have been the height of Wade. A similar claim used to be made for another pair of stones at Goldsborough, 100ft apart.

The greater distance best suits the many tales about Wade. At Saltersgate, between Whitby and Pickering, is the huge hollow of the Hole of Horcum. It has been formed by springs cutting back into the moors for thousands of years. But it is more fun to believe that Wade scooped up a handful of earth and threw it at Bell. And the story becomes even better when you note the 800ft rounded hill of Blakey Topping not far from the giant's crater. What else could this be but Wade's handful of earth, which missed Bell and fell at that spot?

Wade and Bell are credited in folklore with building the castles of Mulgrave and Pickering. Each worked at one castle, sharing a hammer which they tossed backwards and forwards across 17 miles of moor: they gave a warning shout before each throw. Their infant son quickly learned from this example. Left behind on Sleights Moor one day, he accurately aimed a boulder weighing several tons at his mother who was striding across Swarthowe Moor about three miles away. It was the boulder rather than Bell that for ever afterwards bore the imprint of the blow, but sadly this unique missile was broken up for roadmaking about 200 years ago. On Shooting Howe Rigg near Littlebeck, however, is another stone still associated with Bell: from its profile it has earned the name Old Wife's Neck, the wife being Bell.

Wade's Causeway, on Wheeldale Moor, is 16ft wide and more than 1 mile long. Since its Roman origins are not in doubt, it could scarcely have been built by a Saxon chief, let alone a legendary giant. But once again it is pleasant to believe that Bell and Wade built the causeway, including long stretches now under the heather, to link their two castles. And there is yet another story, in which Wade constructed the road as a pathway for Bell, who twice daily needed to milk her giant cow on the moors. For many years a large bone, said to be the rib of this remarkable animal was displayed at Mulgrave. It drew many visitors, who were fond of scratching their initials on the relic. But alas, the exhibit was merely the jawbone of a young whale, put on view as a deliberate joke.

To the casual eye the causeway is a ribbon of small stones. Bell is said to have used her apron to carry these stones, which her husband then scattered on the ground. In one or two places there used to be large piles of stone, supposedly deposited when Bell's apron strings snapped!

The facts about the causeway are no less interesting than these tales. Probably built in the first or second century AD, it was part of a network of Roman roads around Malton. Near the village of Amotherby, the causeway branched from a larger road running to the west. It headed north to the moors and across them to the coast.

Although the road's coastal destination has never been determined, the most likely place is Dunsley, west of Whitby, perhaps the site of a Roman settlement known as Dunum Sinus. The road probably passed near Julian Park farmhouse, Goathland, where a stone was discovered with a Latin inscription saying 'Fifty Vexillary (standard-bearing) soldiers of the 6th Legion, the Victorious'. Transferred to York from Germany in Hadrian's reign (117–38) the 6th legion remained garrisoned in the city until the end of the Roman occupation early in the fifth century. The road might have been built by men of this legion. Its conjectured line to the coast is marked between Aislaby and Egton by a modern stone engraved with the words: Pathway of the Romans.

At Goldsborough, not far from Dunsley, a Roman signal station stood a short distance from the cliff edge. On this site early this century archaeologists uncovered a gruesome tableau. The skeleton of a short, thick-set man was found lying with its skull in the open hearth. He had been stabbed by a second man, whose neck was gripped by the teeth of a large dog. This suggests that Roman rule in the area ended with dramatic suddenness, for if the men had died in a sporadic raid the corpses would surely not have been left in that position.

After the departure of the Romans, the moorland road gradually became overgrown. Its modern history begins with an exploration of it by an eighteenth-century historian named Drake. He heard about the road from a Mr Thomas Robinson of Pickering, and in his book *Eboracum* (1736) he describes his 'great pleasure' in tracing 'this wonderful road ... in many places as firm as it was the first day, a thing the more strange in that not only the distance of time may be considered but the total neglect of repairs and the boggy moors it goes over.' Evidently local people were not quite so enchanted, for Drake reports: 'The country people curse it often; for being almost wholly hid among the ling, it frequently overturns their carts, laden with turf, as they happen to cross it.'

The main surface of the road was flat stones, laid on a bed of earth and gravel that was raised in the centre to provide drainage. In the preserved section all the essential features can be seen, including gutters, culverts and retaining kerbs. The piles of stones supposedly dropped by Bell might simply have been dumps of surplus stone, or perhaps the base of pillars to support wooden bridges across the narrow gills in which the stone was found.

The preserved section was uncovered between 1914 and

1921. It is now cared for by the Department of the Environment. Mr Brian Hugill, of Goathland, has one of the loneliest jobs in Britain, for he is the keeper of the road, weeding it and protecting it from vandals. Reached from either Goathland or Stape (near Pickering), the road can be visited free of charge.

Straddling an unexcavated part of the road 4 miles north of Pickering are the Cawthorne Roman camps. Consisting of four enclosures, the camps cover several acres, and no one is sure why the Romans wanted to amass such military strength at this point. Some people claim that the camps were built to defend the Roman road, others that they were practice camps for soldiers from Malton.

Unfortunately the camps are covered by grass and scrub and are not easy to find among conifer plantations. Cawthorne itself is a vanished village, but by the roadside near one of its two farms is a barn traditionally known as Bibo House. 'Bibo' is the Roman term for an inn, and it could be that the Roman legionaires refreshed themselves at this spot after tramping across the moors on Wade's Causeway nearly 2,000 years ago.

5

ALONG THE COAST

The Staithes' Bonnet

Huddled impressively in the steep cliffs forming the eastern boundary of the North York Moors, the village of Staithes has a notable claim to fame as the place where James Cook, later to become Captain Cook, the great navigator and explorer, was first apprenticed after leaving his parents' home in Great Ayton (see p 206). Unfortunately, the shop in which Cook worked as a grocer's assistant for about eighteen months before beginning a merchant-navy career at Whitby was long ago washed away by the sea. But the cobbled streets and twisting alleyways of the village, with the cottages crowded into every nook and cranny, present a picture that cannot be greatly different from that of Cook's day. And all who visit the village sooner or later ask about a feature that might well have been known to Cook and is still in evidence—the Staithes' bonnet, a highly distinctive head-dress worn by local women.

No one knows exactly when the wearing of the bonnet began, but the date is certainly linked with the important part once played in the local fishing industry by the village women. Their tasks included preparing the fishing lines, which they carried to the boats in coils on their heads. One of Frank Meadow Sutcliffe's famous Whitby photographs shows a line being carried in this way, though by a man, not a woman. The bonnet, fitting closely to the head but broadly flared on both sides, might have evolved as a means of preventing the lines becoming entangled in the women's hair.

Once common all along the Yorkshire coast, the bonnet is now worn only in Staithes. Indeed, the village might well have been the last refuge of the bonnet for more than a century, for when the Cleveland historian John Walker Ord reported on a visit to Staithes' fishquay in the early 1840s, he wrote:

> Numbers of boats had returned laden with the treasures of the deep, now surrounded with stalwart fishermen, proud of their hard-earned spoil. And not the least lively and alert were the sunburnt wives and ruddy daughters, *dressed in their usual showy attire* [my italics].

Was the 'showy attire' peculiar to Staithes? And was the bonnet its distinguishing feature?

One or two women in the village keep alive the craft of bonnet-making. Although the traditional material is lawn—the French linen sometimes grandly called the Cloth of Rheims— most bonnets are today made of cotton. Each bonnet takes about 1yd of material, cut into nine parts. One of the essential features is a double-pleated frill at the front, usually $2\frac{3}{4}$in wide. The bonnet must also have a double crown, emphasising the hard wear it used to receive. It is tied at the back with a bow.

In Victorian days a woman's wardrobe was incomplete without several bonnets. A black bonnet was kept for mourning a close friend or immediate relative while a mauve bonnet was worn for mourning acquaintances or distant relatives. For daily use most women chose a plain white bonnet, although cheerful print bonnets were also popular.

For many years now, people have been predicting the end of the bonnet, gloomily noting that it is worn mostly by older women. But since some of today's wearers must have been young, or even unborn, when the laments first began to be heard, it seems reasonable to conclude there is a steady stream of Staithes' women quietly adopting the bonnet after rejecting

it in their younger days. . . The bonnet is perhaps more endur-
ing than we suppose.

Clearly, however, fewer women wear the bonnet than in the
heyday of the fishing industry. In the first half of the nineteenth
century more than 300 Staithes' men were employed in fishing.
In 1844–5 they manned 45 cobles working locally, plus 31
larger vessels that sailed to Yarmouth each September to join
the herring fleet. Fish was sent to London, Liverpool, Manchester, Leeds, and many other towns. Before the advent of railways, teams of horses, working in relays, carried fish daily to
York market 75 miles away. Fish from Staithes was also
exported to the Mediterranean.

Over-fishing led to reduced yields towards the end of the
nineteenth century. In addition, North Yorkshire's ironstone
boom tempted many men away from the sea. But unlike its
sister villages of Runswick Bay and Robin Hood's Bay, Staithes
has never ceased to support some full-time fishing. Small
boats go potting for crabs and lobsters in summer and work
lines or nets for cod, haddock and other white fish in winter,
The numbers are never high—five boats and twelve men in
1973 for instance—but it will be sad if the day ever dawns when
no fisherman is earning a living at Staithes.

When the fishing industry was at its height, the women not
only prepared and carried lines but mended nets, collected
bait, and cured the fish. The curing was extremely unsavoury
work. After being soaked in brine and pickle, the fish were
spread on the beach to dry. This created a smell described in a
contemporary report as 'offensive to the highest degree'. Perhaps another purpose of the bonnet was to protect the hair from
this odious smell.

Launch the Lifeboat!

Launch the lifeboat! No phrase has ushered in more drama
along the North Yorkshire coast. The region is exceptionally
rich in lifeboat history. At Redcar, just beyond the usual
boundary of this book, you can see the oldest lifeboat in the

world—the *Zetland*. Built at South Shields by Henry Great-
head, the inventor of the lifeboat, she served at the resort from
1802 to 1882, saving 500 lives. Further down the coast, Whitby
proudly displays the last rowing lifeboat used in Britain. In the
ten years before her withdrawal in 1957 she was auxiliary to
Whitby's motor lifeboat, putting to sea 11 times and saving 16
lives. In 1974 she was taken on a national tour as part of the
RNLI's 150th anniversary.

The rocky coast bordering the North York Moors has also
produced a remarkable number of lifeboat epics. In 1881 the
Whitby lifeboat carried out a dramatic overland launch when a
brig, the *Visitor*, foundered in a blizzard off Robin Hood's Bay.
Fifty pairs of horses, supplied in relays by farmers along the
route, shared the task of hauling the boat the 6 miles from
Whitby to the Bay. Women and children held lanterns as men
hacked at the snowdrifts, and the boat was finally manhandled
down an icy slope into the sea. The first rescue attempt failed
when a wave smashed seven of the lifeboat's oars. But the boat
set out again and brought the brig's crew to safety.

This rescue and a comparable one at Lynmouth, Devon, in
1899, are part of lifeboat folklore. But surprisingly little has
been written about the very first overland launch, also by the
men of Whitby. On 28 April 1834, a Newcastle smack, *William*,
was seen drifting mastless towards rocks near Robin Hood's
Bay. One of Whitby's two lifeboats was launched but was unable to cross towering waves at the harbour mouth. It is interesting to recall that this boat used to be suspended from two
stone stanchions that can still be seen on Tate Hill Pier.

With the first boat beaten back, Whitby's second boat,
stationed at Upgang 1 mile north of the town, was yoked to six
horses. Within 45 minutes she arrived at the Bay. Unfortunately, 'night had drawn its sable curtain over the sea', as
a contemporary report poetically noted. But at dawn the
Whitby men achieved a difficult launch. After rescuing two
women passengers they returned to the smack and helped the
crew navigate to Scarborough.

Almost 100 years later another Whitby boat made a possibly

unique inland rescue. When the Esk flooded its banks on 4 September 1931 (virtually repeating a similar flood of 23 July 1930), two elderly women became marooned at Ruswarp. Once again three pairs of horses hauled the Whitby boat through the local streets and lanes. The boat was launched on the Esk just below Ruswarp church, 2 miles from the sea. During the rescue a lifeboatman was swept into the river, but he managed to scramble back into the boat.

In March 1901 the neighbouring Runswick Bay lifeboat was launched by the village women. An impending storm caught the lifeboat crew at sea in their fishing cobles. Apart from the women, only old men and children were left on shore. 'If you can man the boat we can launch her,' the women told the old men. And so it was. Wading waist deep into a turbulent sea, the women gamely tackled a job normally undertaken by twenty vigorous men. Soon the heavy boat was afloat, giving the imperilled cobles a safe escort home.

All these deeds, however, are overshadowed by the stories of the *Rohilla* and Whitby's 1861 Lifeboat Disaster.

The *Rohilla*, a hospital ship, struck rocks at Saltwick Nab, south of Whitby, on Friday, 30 October 1914. Of the 229 people on board, including doctors and nurses, 84 died. The efforts that saved the other 145 were truly heroic. These too began with an unusual launch. High waves at the harbour mouth again prevented the Whitby boat reaching the open sea. The boat was therefore levered through the so-called Spa Ladder, the bridge linking the east pier to the cliff. The ladder takes its name, incidentally, from a mineral spring that once flowed from the cliff at this point, although today's 'Spa' is on the opposite side of the harbour.

Launched from the shore, the lifeboat made two trips and saved thirty-five lives before being forced to retire with holes in her hull. Teams of horses hauled the Upgang boat the 2 miles to Saltwick, but the boat was unable to approach the wreck. Scarborough's lifeboat, towed to the scene by a steam trawler, was similarly helpless, and the Teesmouth motor lifeboat was forced to put back when she was damaged as she left the estuary. A rescue attempt had to be entrusted to the new Tynemouth motor boat, *Henry Vernon*, which faced a 44–mile battle through raging seas even to reach the distressed vessel. The boat accomplished this mammoth task, finally landing survivors 48 hours after the *Rohilla* had foundered. RNLI gold medals were awarded to the Tynemouth cox, Robert Smith, and to his colleague, Captain H. E. Burton, responsible for the brilliant night-time navigation down the largely unlit coast. One of the six medals earned over the years by Whitby lifeboatmen—the largest number for any lifeboat station in the country—went to the Whitby cox Thomas Langlands.

The last survivor of the Whitby crew, John Richardson, died in 1969 aged eighty-one. The *Rohilla*'s steering-wheel and one or two other relics are preserved in the town's lifeboat museum, and in 1972 a Whitby teenager was allowed to keep a silver-plated *Rohilla* coffee jug that he had picked up on the rocks at Saltwick. Most of the vessel was salvaged soon after the disaster, but in 1973 a team of divers recovered the ship's two reserve propellers, kept in the hull. What a splendid monument one of these would have made, mounted on the harbour-side or the cliffs at Saltwick—but sadly both went for scrap. Worth seeing in Whitby cemetery, however, is the memorial to the *Rohilla* dead, dominating a long communal grave.

While the loss of the *Rohilla* is undoubtedly the biggest tragedy to have struck Whitby, a deeper impression on the life of the town was made by the 1861 Lifeboat Disaster, which arrived in the teeth of a tremendous gale on Saturday, 9 February. At 8am a Sunderland brig, the *John and Anne*, was driven ashore near Sandsend Ness. Rowing to the endangered ship, the Whitby lifeboatmen rescued the crew. Soon afterwards a Newcastle collier, *Gamma*, was flung aground. The Whitby boat made a second successful rescue, followed by a third, to the Prussian barque *Clara*; a fourth, to the brig *Utility*; and a fifth, to the schooner *Roe*.

Then, at about 3pm, amid driving snow and sleet, a sixth vessel, the schooner *Merchant*, went aground below the Royal Hotel. It was almost high tide and the sea was mountainous.

'Are you going off?' harbourmaster William Tose asked steersman John Storr. 'Aye, we're going off,' replied Storr. But as the lifeboat approached the schooner's stern, a huge wave surged around the stricken vessel. The wave broke with full force on the lifeboat, which immediately capsized. In the words of a report written soon afterwards: 'Then was beheld by several thousand persons, within almost a stone's throw but unable to assist, the fearful agonies of those powerful men, buffeting with the fury of the breakers, till one by one 12 out of the 13 sank, and only one is saved.' The survivor was Henry Freeman, the only man to wear the RNLI's newly-introduced cork lifejacket.

Freeman told the inquest that tots of rum helped to sustain the men during the long and arduous day. Suggestions that these had rendered half the crew drunk were bitterly resented in Whitby. When a temperance advocate, Thomas Whittaker, suggested that alcohol, offered in 'mistaken kindness', had caused the men to lose 'that self-control and sobriety essential to safety in such a storm', an effigy of him was carried through the town, accompanied by men thrashing it with a whip. The effigy was burned before a cheering crowd on the West Cliff sands.

This barbarism was not the worst of the aftermath. The disaster created ten widows and left forty-four children fatherless. Through an appeal launched with a letter to *The Times*, £5,000 was quickly subscribed. But the widows were given tickets instead of cash, to use in local shops. Inevitably they became known as the 'ticket women'. The grown-up daughter of one of these later recalled that her mother was once sent to a Church of England priest, to have her shoes inspected to see if she deserved another ticket. When the fatherless children reached fourteen, they were given £2 and left to make their way in the world.

The family names of some of the lifeboatmen are still found in Whitby—Harland, Leadley, Storr. A picture of the burly Freeman, wearing his lifejacket, hangs in the Pannet Park Museum, and there is a rather impersonal memorial, in the form of a miniature temple, in the porch of St Mary's Church. The most

eloquent monuments are the gravestones of several of the lifeboat crew by the cliff edge in St Mary's Churchyard, overlooking the sea whose challenge they did not hesitate to meet.

War!

A peculiarity of the North Yorkshire coast is that it has an
historic role in World Wars I and II. On 16 December 1914,
the British Admiralty issued the following announcement:
'German movements of some importance are taking place this
morning in the North Sea. Scarborough and Hartlepool have
been shelled. Our flotillas have at various points been engaged.
The situation is developing.' This was the first, hurried, summary of what is still known in Scarborough and Hartlepool—
and also in Whitby, overlooked by the Admiralty—as The
Bombardment. In a raid of great daring, German warships
stood broadside off the coast and pounded the three towns, killing 166 people and causing widespread damage.

With the war a mere fourteen weeks old, the only previous assault on Britain had been at Yarmouth, where German naval
shells fell harmlessly into the sea. The bombardment of the two
Yorkshire towns plus Hartlepool thereby gave Britain her first
direct taste of world war—foreshadowing the Blitz.

The significance of the event is reflected in the national and
international reaction. The American *Saturday Review* described
the shelling as 'this Satanic Act'. George V sent messages of
sympathy to the Lord-Lieutenants of the North Riding and
County Durham. Winston Churchill, then First Lord of the
Admiralty, despatched letters to the three towns, rich in the
cadences destined to echo round the world: 'We mourn with
you . . . We admire the dignity and fortitude with which Scarborough, Whitby, and Hartlepool have confronted outrage. We
share your disappointment that the miscreants escaped. We
await with patience the opportunity that will surely come.'

On the German side, silver medals were struck for all who
took part in the raid. But the reason for the attack is still not

fully clear. It could have been in retaliation for defeats suffered in the Falkland Isles, or a tactical ploy to persuade Britain to keep her newly trained troops at home. Hartlepool might have been selected because it was within 12 hours' steaming distance of the German fleet's base in Heligoland. The immediate aims were to knock out the shore batteries at the County Durham port and Scarborough, to damage docks and communications, and to lay a minefield.

The Germans assembled a powerful raiding party of 9 cruisers and several destroyers. With about half the vessels standing in reserve, 2 battle cruisers—the mightiest ships in the German fleet—and 1 heavy cruiser, steamed to Hartlepool. The attack opened at 8.10am, and in the following 45 minutes 1,150 shells fell on the town; 119 people were killed, including 15 children and 7 soldiers either on duty or rushing to their posts. As people fled to the countryside 2 British light cruisers and a submarine put out from the port. But the cruisers were no match for the German warships: 1 cruiser was badly crippled and landed 6 dead and several injured sailors at the South Gare Lighthouse Teesmouth.

Sad to relate, the attack was not entirely unexpected, for 2 shore batteries at Hartlepool had been warned by the British war authority to be particularly vigilant between 7am and 8am. But the message was not passed to any of the 4 destroyers based in the port, and when the attack came they were at sea on a routine patrol.

Manned by TA volunteers equipped with three 6in guns, the shore batteries redeemed themselves by killing 80 Germans and wounding 200, without suffering a single casualty of their own. Ten of the German dead were on the heavy cruiser *Blucher* which, to cover the main assault, put up what is believed to have been the first smokescreen of modern warfare.

Meanwhile, in a 20–minute attack beginning at 8.05am 2 more battle cruisers banged about 500 shells into and around Scarborough. Buildings hit included the Grand Hotel, partly occupied by officers of the Yorkshire Hussars, the Balmoral Hotel, the lighthouse, and the parish church of St Mary's.

Firing from the South Bay, the Germans appeared to pay special attention to a range of eighteenth-century red-brick barracks attached to the castle. They perhaps believed, although mistakenly, that the barracks housed soldiers. The range was flattened, and today's visitors to the castle have the German gunners to thank for the exposure of the undercroft of the castle's principal medieval hall at that spot.

Altogether, 19 people were killed and 80 injured in the Scarborough attack, during which the town was filled with black smoke. A railway guard, whose train was waiting in Scarborough, had the presence of mind to collect a large shell cap, which he showed to the astonished citizens of Hull, at the other end of the line!

The attack on Whitby appears to have been an afterthought. At 9am a pair of battle cruisers approached within 500yd of the shore, from which they could be seen keeling over as they fired. On the fiftieth anniversary of the shelling, a former maid at Sandsend recalled that her nose was cut by plaster falling from the ceiling as she served breakfast. Much worse happened, for in a direct hit on Whitby's coastguard station, one of the officers, Fred Randall, was decapitated. In the town, a railway delivery man, William Turnmore, working with his horse and cart, was killed when shrapnel pierced his chest.

Describing the Whitby raid, a newspaper reported: 'The greatest excitement prevailed and many timid persons departed by train, motor, or on foot for inland towns, in search of safety.' The Germans appeared trigger-happy, for many of the 200 shells fired at the port landed far beyond the town: 2 or 3 fell at Ruswarp, 1 zoomed over Sleights Station 4 miles inland, and another broke tiles on a house in Lowdale, Sleights. Back in the town, shells knocked pieces off the west end and north transept of the abbey—battle scars that remain today.

Under cover of the bombardment, the German light cruiser *Kolberg* laid the densest minefield put down anywhere at sea during World War I. Before the field was cleared, the mines claimed 20 ships and more than 100 lives: 11 vessels went down in the first 10 days, including 3 with the loss of 16 lives off Scarborough on Christmas Day.

In World War II the historic coastal action took place in the air. A plaque commemorates the event on an obelisk at the junction of Sleights Lane and the Whitby–Guisborough road: 'The first enemy aircraft to be shot down in England during the second world war fell 80 yards from this tablet on 3rd February, 1940.' The plane was a Heinkel 111—a bomber. A gap in a line of sycamores opposite the obelisk indicates the spot where the plane came to grief. The British pilot who brought it down was Group Captain Peter Townsend, later to become well known through his much publicised romance with Princess Margaret.

Townsend was serving as a young officer at RAF Acklington when he and two fellow pilots were ordered to intercept a plane that had been picked up by radar 60 miles out to sea. Taking off in their Hurricanes they flew fast and low, virtually skimming the waves once the coast was left behind. They soon spotted the Heinkel. Townsend, the leader, immediately gained height and opened fire. The Heinkel's observer was killed instantly and the flight engineer badly wounded. Great courage was displayed by the rear gunner Karl Missy. Although shot in the back and the legs he continued firing as his pilot, Herman Wilms, struggled to keep the crippled plane airborne.

The encounter took place about 2 miles off the coast. Wilms managed to steer the bomber towards land, and as it droned in over the cliffs, losing height all the time, watchers on the ground could clearly see him at the controls. Eventually the bomber came to rest in the snow-covered fields near Sleights, about $1\frac{1}{2}$ miles from the sea. Karl Missy was taken to Whitby Hospital where one of his legs was amputated.

The next day Townsend visited Missy in hospital, and he describes this particular 'strange meeting' in his book, *Duel of Eagles*:

I entered the ward and, on walking straight up to his bed, held out my hand. Turning to me he clasped it with both his until it hurt . . . If he had died I would have been his killer. He said

90

nothing and only looked at me with a pitiful and frightened and infinitely sad expression, in which I thought I could recognise a glimmer of gratitude . . . I held out the bag of oranges and the tin of 50 Players I had brought for him. They seemed poor compensation . . .

Townsend's wartime flying career ended when he was grounded with Messerschmit bullets in his foot. After the war he and Missy met on friendly terms at Missy's home in Rheydt, West Germany. Though neither man had realised it at the time, their dogfight over the North Yorkshire coast had provided the prelude to the Battle of Britain, the Few, and the legend of Britain's Finest Hour.

Old Port, New Port

The happiest story of modern times along the North Yorkshire coast is the revival of Whitby as a port. In the early nineteenth century the town was seventh among the ports of the United Kingdom. With whaling in full swing there was also considerable trade in the export of alum and the import of coal, used in firing the alum shale. The bustle of those days is recalled by one or two wooden capstans surviving on the west pier. They were used for warping-in the sailing ships when there was insufficient wind.

The advent of iron ships and the development of estuaries such as the Tees led to the decline of small harbours such as Whitby. The last wooden ship built in the port, the *Monkshaven*, sailed in 1871, and the following year the harbour was so silted that boys played quoits on gravel in the middle. A few cargo boats trickled in up to the start of World War II, but throughout the first half of this century the work of Whitby as a port was confined mainly to its fishing fleet.

The return of the cargo vessels, the comings and goings of which have brought extra vitality and interest to the town, happened by chance. During a dock strike at Hull in 1955 an importer asked whether Whitby could handle half a dozen potato boats from Belgium. Despite doubts by many people, harbour-master Frank Graves thought the experiment worth a try, and when the six ships successfully unloaded their 2,500 tons of potatoes on Whitby fish quay in June 1955, the rebirth of the old port had begun.

The first outgoing cargo was 545 tons of lime from the Vale of Pickering, despatched to Perth on 11 July 1958. Since then the port has never looked back. In 1964 the local council opened the aptly-named Endeavour wharf, near the railway station, and 5 years later a private wharf on the opposite side of the harbour received its first cargo boat since 1939. Altogether the number of vessels using the port increased from 64 in 1964 to 291 only 8 years later. Today, anyone travelling almost anywhere in North Yorkshire is likely to see evidence of Whitby as a port, for the granite setts bordering most main roads were imported through Whitby from Portugal, over several years beginning in 1971. Other major imports have been timber, paper and chemicals, while exports have included steel, furnace-bricks, doors, and caravans. In 1973 a special shuttle service of vehicles ran between Whitby and a Helmsley sawmill, moving a special import of 600 tons of tree trunks from the Black Forest, the unforeseen harvest of two severe European storms.

The struggle to establish the port was not without its problems and curiosities. Before a radio link was obtained, shore-to-ship signalling was done by the harbour-master flashing his car lights from the seafront. The town's venerable dredger the *Esk*, commissioned in 1936, worked flat out creating a main channel 90ft wide. Her efforts were appreciated on 9 December 1969 when the 1,800 ton Russian ship *Spartak*, the largest vessel yet to use the port, sailed in with timber from the White Sea. She drew 16ft with the high tide obligingly providing just 16ft 2in.

Among those delighted to see this ship berth was Mr Brian Whitaker, a Whitby bus driver. In 1958 he began photographing the cargo boats in the port. By 1973 his pictures filled thirteen large albums, a unique and valuable record. In his eagerness to get a good shot he once fell off the quayside on to the deck of a fishing boat, and it was not unusual to see him sprinting along the harbourside to reach a favoured vantage point. The appeal of the ships is not hard to appreciate, for they make a fine sight riding high among the harbourside buildings, or breasting the waves at the harbourmouth as they embark on their voyages across the North Sea.

In 1977 work began on a scheme to enlarge the harbour, enabling it to handle about 600 ships a year. The scheme involves dredging mudflats in the upper harbour and reclaiming about $7\frac{1}{4}$ acres of land. The upper harbour channel will be widened and the Endeavour Wharf extended, with a much needed lay-by berth. Extra space will also be created for the 300 yachts that regularly use the harbour, and there is talk of building a new quay for the fishing fleet, usually numbering about 15 keel boats and between 25 and 30 cobles. Altogether, the harbour activity that gives so much pleasure to visitors to the ancient port will not be reduced.

Frank Meadow Sutcliffe

Frank Meadow Sutcliffe wrote that the Whitby district always offered 'something to beguile'. In capturing this he produced photographs of near genius. For many people it is impossible to view the scenes he depicted except through his eyes. The knot of visitors usually to be found gazing through the window of the Sutcliffe Gallery, the Whitby shop that sells Sutcliffe prints, testifies to the popularity of his work. Period charm is only part of the appeal, for the humanity of Sutcliffe's work is eternal and universal. I also believe that the success of his photographs depends at least partly on a paradox. While the lifestyles of the late-Victorian and Edwardian world evoked by Sutcliffe have vanished, the backgrounds to many of his photographs remain essentially unchanged. The ability to transpose oneself where Sutcliffe shows the sou'westered fishermen or ploughboys pausing for a gossip provides a tang that would be absent if Whitby and its nearby countryside had changed beyond recognition this century.

93

Sutcliffe was born at Headingley, Leeds, in 1853. His father was a landscape painter with an interest in etching and lithography. Frank enjoyed experimenting with the printing apparatus, being particularly fond of creating images of the Leeds' fogs.

In 1870, shortly before the death of Mr Sutcliffe, the family moved for a healthier climate to Ewecote Hall, an interesting house west of Whitby. Other occupants at different times have been the Duchess of Buckingham, who lived there while supervising the building of Mulgrave Castle; and Captain Titus Oates, the 'very gallant gentleman' of Captain Scott's ill fated expedition to the Antarctic.

In 1874, acting on a suggestion made earlier by his father, Sutcliffe decided to try and earn his living by photography. With the intention of becoming a society photographer he moved with his young wife, a North Yorkshire girl named Eliza Duck, to fashionable Tunbridge Wells. The venture was a failure and within a year the Sutcliffes were back in Whitby. Sutcliffe then opened a studio in a former jet workshop, and thus began one of Britain's greatest photographic careers.

Sutcliffe's efforts raised photography to an art despite his own unflattering opinion of the activity. 'A photograph is a very shallow thing compared with a painting,' he wrote. He also complained that photography was 'born of poor and not too admirable parents—necessity and laziness'. There is evidence that early in his career he strove to make his photographs serve as substitutes for paintings, and there are several instances in his work where the silhouettes of ships or the subtleties of skies suggest a Victorian working in oils.

It is often overlooked that the staple fare of Sutcliffe's business was family portraiture. Dusty albums contain many examples of Sutcliffe's work in this sphere, but the results are usually unremarkable. Sutcliffe's skill flourished when he set out to record the daily life of Whitby and its rural hinterland. The novelty of the expeditions can hardly be overstated, nor their difficulties. Sutcliffe's camera was a heavy mahogany affair that extended to 3ft and was capable of taking plates measuring 24 by 18in. He also carried with him a large tent, as a darkroom for on-the-spot developing. Producing six pictures a day was hard work.

A common misconception about Sutcliffe's photographs is that they capture spontaneous scenes or incidents. Although he helped to pioneer the 'natural' school of photography his pictures are all carefully composed. Like all other photographers of his day he was precluded by his cumbersome equipment from taking the snapshot, the quick slice of life. Sutcliffe arranged the people in his photographs to achieve the desired effect. But the result is a superb example of art hiding art: very often, Sutcliffe's photographs are more 'true' than the truth that suggested the picture!

What Sutcliffe did mostly eschew were photographs using theatrical props—artifical from beginning to end. A rare example of such a picture is included in an anthology of his work published by the Sutcliffe Gallery. It is a re-creation of a smugglers' den, with fishermen dressed for the part.

A pleasing feature of Sutcliffe's work is the titling of his photographs, for example, 'Stern Realities', for a rear view of boys peering over the harbour wall, or 'Limpets', for two girls on a rock. The most famous title is 'Water Rats', describing nude boys playing around a boat. Sutcliffe took this picture in 1886 when he saw the boys bathing. He gave the youngsters pennies to remain in the water while he organised the picture. The Prince of Wales, later Edward VII, saw a print of the photograph in an exhibition and ordered a copy, which was hung in Marlborough House. But Whitby's clergymen were less pleased. They excommunicated Sutcliffe for exhibiting a work 'to the corruption of the young of the other sex'.

With World War I bringing a ban on outdoor photography along the east coast, Sutcliffe's unique record of Whitby life, spanning forty years and amounting to the most complete pictorial record ever made of an English town, came to an end. After selling his business in 1922 he became curator of Whitby's Pannet Park Museum. His original studio, 25 Skinner Street, is today a fruit shop.

Although Sutcliffe never worked in the Sutcliffe Gallery, the premises were first opened as a photographic shop by Sutcliffe's assistant Tom Gillat, who took over the business on Sutcliffe's retirement. The continuing availability of the Sutcliffe prints owes much to the careful preservation of his original plates by the Whitby Literary and Philosophical Society.

Despite winning more than sixty medals in cities around the world, Sutcliffe felt bitter throughout much of his working life at what he regarded as his lack of recognition. In 1935, however, he received Britain's highest photographic honour when he was elected an Honorary Fellow of the Royal Photographic Society. Second only to Captain Cook as Whitby's most famous adopted son, he died in 1941 aged eighty-seven. But to many people his spirit lives on, and in the ghauts and yards of old Whitby it would be no surprise to come across the man himself, arranging a doorstep group discussing the latest news.

6

AROUND THE MOORS

The Moorland Watercourses

On view in a showcase in Ryedale Museum, Hutton-le-Hole is
a surveyor's level resembling an antique telescope. Behind it is
a large map of the countryside between Lastingham and Old
Byland. Together they tell the story of a minor masterpiece of
the moors—a series of man-made watercourses that perform
the impossible by scaling an escarpment which reaches heights
of up to 200ft in places.

The watercourses were created to convey drinking water to a
number of moorland villages. The need for the system is made
clear by a visit to Fadmoor and Gillamoor, poised on the raised
tip of the Tabular Hills north of Kirbymoorside. Almost all the
natural flow of water is away from the villages, either down the
steep scarp to the central moorlands or along the more gentle
slope towards the Vale of Pickering. Why these and one or two
similarly 'dry' villages were built in such positions is an interesting question: perhaps the advantages of a good soil out-
weighed the lack of running water.

For centuries, supplies were improvised by the collection of
rainwater in tanks and ponds. In the mid-eighteenth century,
however, Joseph Foord, a self-taught surveyor from Kirbymoorside, decided to provide a running supply. The only possible source was the higher moors to the north. There was no
serious difficulty in bringing water to the foot of the Tabular

97

Hills, for this was a downward journey all the way. But the water had then to be persuaded to climb the escarpment. The surveyor's level in Ryedale Museum is the instrument used by Foord to achieve this miracle. The map shows the waterways he made.

There were six in all. In 1747 Foord brought water over the cliff to Fadmoor and Gillamoor. He then devised a watercourse for Nawton and Beadlam, which cleverly conveyed water from one dale to another. In 1758 he completed another supply, to Griff, near Rievaulx, and the following year he engineered a supply to Carlton, near Helmsley. He also provided watercourses for Pockley and Lastingham, the latter again linking two neighbouring valleys.

The secret of Foord's success lay in his brilliant observation that the entire bulk of the Tabular Hills tilts down towards the coast—ie eastwards. The more westerly one travels the higher is the foot of the escarpment above sea-level. The effect of this can be appreciated by tilting a pencil horizontally between the thumb and forefinger, with the left end higher than the right. For each village to be served, Foord found the critical point at which the base of the escarpment is higher than the village. He then sloped his watercourse across the face of the escarpment with a very slight fall all the way—and lo! the trick was performed.

Although the idea was simple, the surveying measurements were very fine. The Nawton watercourse falls only about 100ft in 7 miles. This supply takes its water from a spring at Piethorn on Bilsdale East Moors. It soon swings away from its destination, crossing Bonfield Gill by a stone aqueduct. There it receives more water, tapped from the gill by an artificial cut. It then steals around the front of Birk Nab to slip unobtrusively from Riccaldale to Bransdale.

Foord's ingenuity was once excellently seen at Cow House Bank, on the East Moors road into Bransdale. By optical illusion the Carlton Watercourse at that point appears to run uphill, which it very nearly does. Unfortunately, this interesting spectacle might soon be lost, for this watercourse has

98

been fighting a losing battle with nature since 1960 when, in common with the other watercourses in the area, it was replaced by a piped supply, pumped mainly from Ness, near Nunnington.

Farming has now almost totally obliterated the longest watercourse which runs to Griff. On a route of more than 10 miles it twice passed under the main Bilsdale road. The Carlton watercourse was almost as long, rambling for about 9 miles to reach the escarpment. Forestry has disturbed one of its special features, an embankment about 100yd long and between 5ft and 6ft high to traverse boggy ground at Roppa Edge. Also vanished is a hollow tree trunk, by which the 6–mile Pockley watercourse crossed a ravine. The shortest watercourse, which was powerful enough to drive a mill, served Lastingham, running for about 1 mile from Loskey Beck, north of the Rosedale/Hutton-le-Hole road, to Commomile Farm.

The waterways quickly became very important. The Nawton channel was extended to serve Skiplam, Welburn and Wombleton, and the Carlton course eventually ran to Helmsley. The original Gillamoor and Fadmoor scheme was linked with Kirbymoorside, with an agreement that the town should take seven-tenths of the supply, Gillamoor two-tenths and Fadmoor one-tenth. Holes of appropriate size were cut in the terminal reservoir, to ensure that each community received exactly its due share.

The watercourses themselves were little more than ditches, about 12in wide and 12in deep. They were easily blocked, or damaged by cart wheels, and illegal tapping was not unknown. To prevent loss by seepage the channel was lined with clay, but this sometimes cracked, causing what was known as 'a sink'. A Kirbymoorside enclosure award of 1788 includes an order that a public meeting should be held every year to appoint a surveyor of the local waterways. This officer became known as the waterman, and in the nineteenth century one of them, George Wright, lodged at the White Horse Inn, Beadlam. His tools included an iron scoop for cleaning the channel. A crisis developed one winter when the Nawton supply was frozen for a long period. Consumers withheld their rates, from which the water-man received his wages. He retaliated by refusing to work, but fortunately the dispute was short-lived.

The speed with which these unique watercourses have slipped towards oblivion is illustrated by the disappearance of the Carlton watercourse from the 1in edition of the Ordnance Survey map little more than ten years after the supply was still a vital local lifeline. It is also sad to report that when members of the Helmsley group of the Yorkshire Archaeology Society carried out repairs to the Bonfield Gill aqueduct in 1964, the Department of the Environment refused their request to have the structure listed as of historic importance. The aqueduct is still there, and so are many miles of watercourses, although masked by heather. With the aid of old maps it makes an interesting day's tramp to trace the route of the Carlton watercourse. The terrain is rough but the walker is well rewarded with the sight of a piece of moorland handiwork that deserves to be remembered.

Farndale

Easily the best known valley of the North York Moors, Farndale owes its fame to the daffodils that bloom almost from one end of the dale to the other. In 1972, according to a census by the national park authority, 56,000 people visited the valley during the brief daffodil season. Many embarked on the most popular daffodil walk, a 1½-mile trek between the hamlets of Low Mill and Church Houses. At times, congestion on this path is so great that queues form at stiles. There are high heels, poodles and push-chairs. Amateur cameramen bestride the flowers to record family groups, while arm-banded wardens, some with walkie-talkies, mingle among the crowd. But large concentrations of daffodils can be visited away from this over-used path, and beyond them lies a Farndale that few people know, full of beauty and interest.

The name Farndale is often taken to mean 'fern valley'. A more likely derivation is from the Gaelic word 'fearna' meaning

Plates 8 and 9 The village scene: *(above)* Staithes, which has maintained a tenacious hold on full-time fishing. The shop in which Captain Cook worked stood near the houses on the extreme left, when the street extended further than it does now. The Cod and Lobster pub, jutting into the harbour nearby, had to be rebuilt after the coastal storms of 1953; *(below)* Beck Hole, with its cottages grouped exquisitely around a green on which quoits is played.

Plates 10 and 11 Mementoes of man: *(above)* the White Horse peers into his village of Kilburn, where oak lies seasoning for the Robert Thompson furniture craftsmen. Their showroom is the half-timbered building in the centre, with their workshop on the extreme right; *(below)* the amazing Bulmer Stone at Westerdale, part of the moorland's extensive heritage of inscribed stones

alder, for the alder tree is still common in the dale while ferns have probably never been prolific. The equally attractive name of Farndale's river, the Dove, probably has its origin in the Celtic word 'dubo', the black or shady stream. High up on the west side of the valley, by the roadside, is a large boulder known as the Duffin Stone. This might identify one of the two original forest clearings at Farndale, named as Duvanesthaut in a Rievaulx Abbey charter of 1154.

Several features of Farndale are described elsewhere in this book—the Hangman Stone (p 107), the Horn Nab earthwork (p 23), and the dale's cruck houses (p 179). The dale also has important links with ironstone. On Harland Moor are examples of the Bell Pits, the early method of winning ore by digging what became bell-shaped holes. Several hundred years after these workings were abandoned the valley was drawn into the Victorian ironstone boom. A spur was built from the Rosedale Railway (see p 125) and ore from a mine at Low Blakey was hauled up an incline. Although a miner commented that there was 'not enough iron to nail your boots', the venture survived for thirty years from 1850 to 1880 and the remains of two buildings, including the winding-house, can still be seen south of Blakey Bank.

Coal and jet have also been mined in Farndale, the former at pits on Rudland Rigg and Blakey Ridge, the latter near Lendersfield House in the north-western corner of the dale. At the opposite end of the valley a large cluster of buildings at Lowna Farm testifies to the farm's 100-year history as a tannery and mill. Up to 1914 half the bark from Helmsley's Duncombe Park estate was handled there, with special wheelbarrows for running it to six soaking pits. The mill not only ground corn but crushed bone to produce meal. On my last visit the corn-grinding stones were still in place and a hand-operated sluice in working order. The remains of the tannery shafting and drive gear could also be seen.

The classic way to sample Farndale is to walk across the moors from the north and follow as many paths as possible to Lowna. Perhaps the best route lies past the ruined Middle

Head Farm, the highest dwelling in the dale. Once known as Middlehovet, this was the second original forest clearing in the valley. Unoccupied since 1920, in the Middle Ages the cottage sheltered a hermit, and it is also the centre of an astonishing tale concerning a farmer's daughter who answered a knock and found a fat woman on the doorstep. The woman entered the house and said she wished to wait for her husband. But as the visitor dozed in a chair, the farmer's daughter, who was alone, noticed trousers beneath the skirt. She promptly poured boiling fat down the intruder's throat and dumped the body on the manure heap. That night the girl, still alone, heard someone calling, 'Are you there, Fatty?' The girl flung open the window and shouted that Fatty was on the midden. The next day the body had disappeared, but years later, so the story says, a skull was found in a hole in the nearby hillside.

Many other Farndale tales involve witches and sprites. On the moors above West Gill is a tumulus named Obtrusch Roque—Hobgoblin's Heap. It is said that a farmer at West Gill was so plagued by the local sprite that he decided to move. With his possessions on a cart he passed a neighbour who called out: 'I see thou's flittin'.' A voice answered from the family churn, 'Aye we's flittin',' to which the farmer replied: 'Well, if thou's flittin' we might as well gan yam ageean.' An old Farndale poem tells of Elphi, a bandy-legged dwarf, and the strength of the hobgoblin tradition is also indicated by a former local description of flint arrowheads as 'elf darts'.

The special experience of Farndale is the valley's daffodils. They bloom for 7 miles in the dale, from just below Middle Head to the termination of the dale at Lowna. And they even persist a mile or two beyond Lowna, to where the Dove enters a limestone gorge at Yoadwath.

Unknown to many people, wild daffodils also bloom in woods near Sinnington, immediately east of Farndale. Upper Bilsdale also has several expanses of daffodils, mostly planted by a landowner in the early 1970s. But Farndale has literally millions of blooms. Often, the drifts cover several hundred square yards. A skilled botanist has identified seven or eight different varieties of the flower, most of them characterised by a short stalk and narrow trumpet. No one knows how they arrived in the valley. A claim is sometimes made that the first bulbs were planted by Father Nicholas Postgate, an itinerant seventeenth-century priest (see p 163). But although Postgate is known to have liked flowers, there is nothing to link him directly with Farndale or her daffodils. And there is no evidence to support a popular theory that the flowers were introduced by the monks of Rievaulx Abbey.

Throughout the first half of this century the daffodils were ruthlessly plundered. Market traders picked large bunches to sell in industrial towns, and after World War I motorists began filling their car boots with blooms and bulbs. The pillage was halted in 1953 when 2,000 acres of the valley were designated a nature reserve. Notices now warn of the penalties for picking the flowers or removing the bulbs. Most people respect the law and warnings for misbehaviour are largely unneeded.

Since the imposition of the ban, however, argument has arisen over whether the plants benefit or suffer by the restriction. In 1969 the Nature Conservancy Council launched a scientific study in which the fieldwork is undertaken by secondary-school children from Pickering. The study is still continuing, but some useful research was carried out in the early 1960s by Mr Richard Bell, head warden of the North York Moors National Park. Marking out various groups of daffodils and counting the blooms each year, Mr Bell found that broadly, while some groups of daffodils advance others recede, perhaps following a cycle governed by available nutrients in the soil. Both Mr Bell and the Nature Conservancy Council insist that casual personal observation is highly unreliable. A visitor may be disappointed when a well remembered patch of daffodils is not as impressive one year as another. But he does not recall a small group of blooms that has subsequently increased. Besides, as Mr Bell shrewdly points out, the daffodils survived hundreds, if not thousands of years before mass picking began.

If a midweek day is chosen, the walk between Low Mill and Church Houses makes a fine introduction to the daffodils.

Worth noting en route are two massive pairs of gateposts near the High Mill. One of the posts is engraved with the date 1826 and three sets of initials—probably of the men who positioned the posts. The size of the posts indicates why the men would wish to commemorate their day's work.

Until a window was boarded up a year or two ago, the High Mill also offered a view of a blacksmith's forge, little changed since it was last used in 1939. The dusty tableau is probably still there—bellows, hearth, anvil and all. And don't miss the detached sandstone privy in High Mill garden, a piece of North Yorkshire vernacular architecture well worth preserving!

For Sunday visitors to the daffodils, the best walk is one that starts at a car park near Lowna Farm. It has the merit of paths on both banks of the river and offers perhaps the prettiest views of the daffodils, although the blooms are massed more extensively near Church Houses. The walk can include a visit to a little known Quaker burial ground, on the west side of the river not far from the car park. It is marked by a plaque stating that between 1675 and 1837, 114 Quakers were buried there. The walk may also be extended to Rawson Sike, near Low Mill, with views of daffodils well away from the river.

Between 1967 and 1970 a furious row raged over a scheme to create a reservoir in Upper Farndale, above Church Houses. Fortunately, in my view, a Select Committee of the House of Commons rejected the plan, which does not now figure in any proposals. While it is true that neither of the two popular daffodil walks would have been drowned, a large part of the nature reserve would have been sacrificed. There was also a danger that the reservoir would have made Farndale almost as busy throughout the summer as it is during the daffodil season. Thankfully, the valley is tranquil and restful for most of the year, adding to the pleasure of discovering its many riches.

Stories in Stone

Scrambling on the moors near Ingleby Greenhow a year or two ago I came across an unusual stone seat, partly obscured by bracken and young larch trees. Hewn from a single boulder and able to accommodate only one person, it is neatly engraved with the name and date: 'Lady Mary Ross 1837'. I later discovered that Mary Ross was the eldest daughter of the 21st Earl of Kildare. As the wife of Lt Gen Sir Charles Ross she had a daughter who, early in the nineteenth century, married Sir William Foulis of Ingleby Manor. No doubt Lady Mary visited her daughter and son-in-law at the manor, and the stone seat, commanding a fine view of the Cleveland Hills and the countryside stretching to the Yorkshire Dales, probably marks a favourite spot on one of her walks.

The Mary Ross seat is one of scores of 'standing stones' in the moors, many with stories to tell. The first boundary stone north of Lowna Bridge, Farndale, for instance, is known as the Hangman Stone. A man carrying home a slaughtered sheep is said to have accidentally killed himself when he sat down to rest at the stone. Apparently he balanced the carcass on top of the stone, and it slipped down the other side, strangling the man by the string fastened across its legs.

Several other moorland stones have tragic associations. At Tarn Hole in Tripsdale, a tributary valley of Bilsdale, is the Buckingham Stone. According to an old legend, in 1687 Helmsley's Duke of Buckingham contracted a cold after resting on this stone during a hunt with the Bilsdale hounds, and subsequently died in Kirbymoorside. Alexander Pope described his death as being 'in the worst inn's worst room'. The building, still named Buckingham House, is now a private residence, near the King's Head Hotel.

Among moorland stones set up as memorials is a rough pillar between Lealholm and Stonegate Mill. Engraved on it is the stark message: 'Found Dead. William Shaw of Lealholmside, March 13th, 1898. Aged 89 years.' Some people say that Shaw perished in a snowstorm, others that he died while burning heather. A Lealholm man with a less formal memorial is John Castillo, a dialect poet sometimes called 'the bard of the dales'. Castillo's grave can be seen in the Wesleyan cemetery at Pickering, the town in which he died in

1845. But Castillo, a skilled stone mason, once carved his name on a large flat rock known as the Dancing Stone, east of Danby Head. After his death someone added: 'Neu Hees deead.'

The largest group of rocks in the national park is the Wainstones, on Hasty Bank near Great Broughton. 200 years ago historians were greatly perplexed by the following marks on a fallen slab.

ꓘOJꓒOJ2

ㄒ ⱯOⱲJⴖᒑㄒD

The Rev John Graves made the inscription part of the frontispiece of his 1808 *History of Cleveland*. But eventually it was deciphered as an elaborate love message: RO WOOING TD 1712. I have looked in vain for this inscription, but a stone with rather similar markings awaits the diligent searcher in the unpleasantly-named Snotterdale, an offshoot of Scugdale, near Swainby, chiefly notable as an abundant source of loose jet.

Back on the Wainstones, two carvings are particularly worth noting among the lower rocks—about 100yd below the main group on the north side. One, dating from 1874, shows either two hounds or a hound pursuing a fox, both about 2ft long. The other, carved in the 1970s, features the modern evangelical message 'One Way', with a large hand pointing dramatically skywards.

The name Wainstones is itself often the subject of debate. The word is sometimes said to mean 'the stones by the way', for a well preserved pedlar's track, best seen above Kirby village, crosses the moors nearby. There is also a claim that the name is derived from the Saxon verb 'wanian' to howl, making the Wainstones 'the stones of lamentation'. This could refer to the wind among the stones or perhaps indicate that the Wainstones were once a burial ground. A 1642 description of the Helmsley estate records the Wainstones as the Whinnstones. This comes close to the known use of the outcrop as a quarry: in 1819 the Enclosure Commissioners ordered that a 21ft roadway had to be constructed for access to the quarry. This roadway, running around the Bilsdale side of the hill, can still be traced.

On the central massif of the moors a mile or two to the east of the Wainstones are a large number of named stones—Badger Stone, Cheese Stone, etc. The best known are the Face Stone and the Hand Stone, by the Lyke Wake Walk track on Urra Moor. The face, crudely carved on the Face Stone, is often said to be Celtic and to commemorate a burial at that spot. But the carving could equally be frivolous, for there are many similar examples on the moors. By the Wainstones quarry road, for instance, is an excellent carving of an Egyptian head, cut only a few years ago but already weathered to match the surrounding rock. And particularly worth noting on the Ingleby Incline (see p 125) is a carving of a man in a stovepipe hat. This could be the work of a navvy who helped to construct the incline, perhaps caricaturing a railway director.

The Urra Moor handstone is probably one of a profusion of waymarkers erected after the North Riding magistrates, meeting at Northallerton on 2 October 1711, ordered that stone guideposts be put up in every parish. Several of these stones can be seen on Blakey Ridge and Rudland Rigg, generally with the place names spelt phonetically.

Distinct from the guideposts on Rudland Rigg is the so called Cammon or Common Stone, bearing a series of strange hieroglyphics. These are Hebrew for hallelujah and they were probably engraved by the Rev Emmanuel Strickland, a nineteenth-century priest at Ingleby Greenhow. Strickland is known to have carved a longer inscription, in Greek and Latin as well as Hebrew, on Bransdale Mill. It is also possible that he is responsible for the quaint carvings of animals on the capitals in Ingleby Greenhow parish church, although local people insist they are much older. The view from the Cammon Stone explains his expression of joy.

Close to the Lealholm–Rosedale road on Glaisdale Moor are two stone markers, set 13yd apart. One of them is engraved Hart's Leap, and they are said to mark the last gigantic leap of a hunted deer. Not far away in Glaisdale Head a post is inscribed Peathill Road, obviously identifying a route by which peat was

109

brought down from the moors. With peat and turves (the top layer of a heathery moor) still burned in some moorland homes, rights to cut the fuel are jealously guarded. A few years ago this gave rise to one of the oddest of moorland 'standing stones', at Goathland. When a cottage was being demolished to make way for a new house, the old fireplace was carefully preserved to retain the peat-cutting rights which the owner believed were attached directly to the hearth. Today, the blackened side walls and massive hearth-stone of the old fireplace stand in the garden of the house named Friar' Close, converted into a seat!

Glaisdale's Peathill Stone is engraved with the date 1735 and several personal names. Among them is Thomas Harwood, who might be called the king of the standing stones. He used them as other men might have used parchment—to record legal transactions. On a gatepost in Glaisdale Head appears the order: 'Francis Hartus to repare this yat and yattstead TH 1737.' Hartus was probably a tenant farmer whose duties were thus made clear. On another gatepost, a longer but damaged inscription says: 'Go with cart and carig any tim(e) without hindrance . . . It is in writing Francis Hartus hand and seal 1737 TH.' Since the earliest-known Harwood stone is dated 1699 we can deduce that he was inscribing his stones for more than thirty years. His home might have been what is now a ruined house between Glaisdale Head and Glaisdale village, the lintel of which bears the initials TMH and the date 1726.

Harwood's stones are not the only ones engraved to settle the law. A stone near Goathland is inscribed: 'Boundary Determined at York Assizes 1813.' And at Cringle Moor, a quarry face was used to record a change of ownership in the local Dromonby estate in 1732. Responsibility fell to five people, each of whom is named on the rock, which is the only instance in the national park of a quarry face serving as a boundary marker. The inscription is completed with a Latin phrase that is one of three known to me on rocks in the moors. The second is only a yard or two away and probably also relates to the often complicated affairs of the Dromonby estate. The inscription reads: *Tempus*

Omnia Explora Negotium (Time settles all business).

The third Latin inscription is to be found on the huge Shipstone in Tripsdale. Engraved very boldly are the words: *Dei Plena Sunt Omnia* (All things are full of God). Dated 1849 in Roman numerals the inscription was probably the work of a Bilsdale farmer, who signed himself Johannes Cervus, Billsvallensis.

In 1714 a large moorland boulder near Falling Foss Waterfall, Littlebeck, was hollowed out to become a charming folly. A Gothic doorway leads into a grotto or shelter, with a stone bench running around the wall. Known as the Hermitage, the folly was made by a sailor named Jeffrey on the orders of a Littlebeck schoolmaster called George Chubb, whose initials appear on the shelter. The work was part of a scheme devised by Chubb for improving the grounds of nearby Newton House for a new owner, Jonas Brown. An obelisk at Newton House (so-called because it was originally 'Tommy Newton's sheep house'), commemorates Brown. Visitors to the Hermitage should not miss the seats carved from solid stone on top of the cave: they are surprisingly comfortable.

Not all engraved stones are old. In the early 1970s excellent likenesses of grouse were cut into the walls of shooting butts on Warren Moor, Kildale, by a local man, Roland Close. And on Trennet Bank, Chop Gate, walkers are now wearing a path to a beautifully sited headstone placed there in memory of Joan Hutton-Wilson, of Bilsdale Hall, who was killed in a road accident in 1969.

A modern stone of exceptional interest stands by the eastern road into Great Fryup Dale. This road formerly had six gates in its first mile. Tired of having to open and close five of them every day, John Tinsley, a worker on the Lealholm estate, decided that the gates should be removed. He invited subscriptions from agricultural firms whose travellers also used the road. The gates were duly removed and, at John's request, Frank Weatherill of Danby set up the commemorative stone.

The inscription says:

111

Six gates in next mile a nuisance proved.
Helped by kind donors, tenants and others
had them removed.
USE WELL TIME SAVED

More enigmatic is the stone in a field behind the church at
Nether Silton. It is engraved with this conundrum:

HTGOMHS

TBBWOTGWWG

TWOTEWAHH

ATCLABWHEY

AD 1765

AWPSAYAA

The explanation is that each letter is the initial of a word.
The full inscription, carved on the instruction of Silton's Squire
Hickes in the eighteenth century, says:

Here the grand old manor house stood. The black beams were
oak, the great walls were good; the walls of the east wing are
hidden here; a thatched cottage like a barn was here erected year
AD 1765; a wide porch spans a yard and alcove.

But my favourite among all moorland stones is a pillar
mounted in the garden of a cottage at Westerdale. Almost every
square inch is filled with lettering, but with a little difficulty a
complete narrative can be worked out, beginning like this:
'1727. In this year it was my true intent to make here a lasting
monument, to show Thy mercies everywhere around and
save u(s) when no mankind are to be found. Of this have I
had large expieryance.'

The 'expieryance' turns out to have been a shipwreck,
hinted at by four ships carved around the base. The inscription gives the details:

Thomas Bulmer who lived here has often crossed the Main to
many foreign shores, then Germany, Holland, France and

112

Spain. Wrecked at length his frail bark, the hopeful anchors cast, is now unrigged and here lyeth moored fast. Tossed on rough seas on broken pieces of the ship until daybreak, then they escaped all safe to land. Remember man, thy sail on sea, short it must be, and then be turned to dust.

In further inscriptions Bulmer adds that his ship was a 'providence of faith, hope and charity'. More of his story may be found in Westerdale churchyard where a gravestone, obviously carved by the same hand as the stone in the garden, records the death, also in 1727, of a seventeen-year-old boy named Bulmer, who was perhaps Thomas's son. Bulmer's own gravestone, featuring a skull and crossbones, stands alongside. Both these stones have been moved at some time to their present very forlorn position against the rear wall of the church, and it would be a nice gesture to have them set up where they can be easily seen.

Danby and District

Standing for the first time on the moorland height known as Danby Beacon, Canon John Christopher Atkinson saw before him what he described as 'the long valley running east and west . . . with dale after dale opening into it from its southern side'. He considered the view 'one of the loveliest it had ever been my lot to behold. With colour, contrast and contour, soaring hill and deepening dale, abrupt nab end and craggy wood all claiming notice at once, the scene was something more than simply beautiful.'

This remains a good description of the Danby region of Upper Eskdale, an area forever associated with Canon Atkinson, its vicar from 1847 to 1900. The canon became famous through his book *Forty Years in a Moorland Parish*, in which the above passage appears. First published in 1891, the book is valuable today more for its impressions of moorland life a century ago than for its now often outdated interpretation of local history. The canon writes in a robust, readable style, well illustrated by this account of his first visit to his new parish church:

> Suffice to say that my conductor, the 'minister', entered with-
> out removing his hat, walked through the sacred building and up
> to the holy table with his hat still on. Although I had seen many
> an uncared-for church and many a shabby altar, I thought I had
> reached the farthest extreme now. The altar-table was not only
> rickety, and with one leg shorter than the other, and besides that
> mean and worm-eaten, but it was covered with what it would
> have been a severe and sarcastic libel to call a piece of green
> baize; for it was in rags. And even that was not all. It was covered
> thickly over with stale crumbs. It seemed impossible not to crave
> some explanation of this; and the answer to my inquiry was as
> nearly as possible in the following terms: 'Why it is the Sunday
> school teachers. They must get their meat (food) somewhere and
> they gets it here.' . . . Such was the parish church and such its
> reverend but hardly reverent minister. And he was but one of a
> pair, for his brother was parish clerk and schoolmaster; and the
> first time I had to take a funeral, on arriving at the church a little
> in advance of the hour fixed, I became aware of a strong perfume
> of tobacco smoke; and there inside the church I saw the clerk sit-
> ting in the sunny embrasure of the west window, with his hat on
> of course, comfortably smoking his pipe.

Born at Goldhanger, Essex, the canon was 33 when he arrived at Danby. His 3 wives bore him 13 children, but none of the family now lives in the area. Very few people remember the canon, and the only impression that survives is of the old man, frail but still upright. Danby's present vicar, the Rev David Adam, once told me: 'He was the complete Victorian clergy-man. Right to the end men lifted their hats to him, and children curtsied.'

In *Forty Years* the canon estimates that he walked about 70,000 miles in the course of his ministry. Much of this tramping would be to and from Danby church, 1½ miles from the village. There is speculation that an earlier Danby, now a 'lost' village, existed near the church. In any case, until the growth of the present village, mainly in the eighteenth and nineteenth centuries, the church was well placed to serve the surrounding farms. A stone cross in the churchyard marks the canon's grave and a plaque commemorates him inside the church.

Another notable tablet commemorates Samuel Raybanks, for whom the number 9 obviously had some significance: he left 9d (about 4p) a week to be paid on the ninth of each month to 9 poor persons, selected from twice 9 candidates.

Danby also has a castle, which is some distance from the village, near the road to Fryup. Built about 1300, it presents a massive appearance from the main road through Eskdale. Its builder and first owner was William Latimer, and later owners included the Nevilles of Raby, County Durham. Their coat-of-arms can be seen on the wall near the Fryup road.

The conversion of the castle into a farm, plus the complete disappearance of the western range containing the main entrance, makes the original plan hard to appreciate. But the castle was a landmark in the history of castle architecture. It was one of the first to be constructed around a central courtyard, dispensing with the keep and relying entirely on very strong outer walls. The pioneering design included four extremely large projecting angle towers. One of these can still be seen, jutting sharply from the main wall, with the farmhouse added to it. Such bold projections proved difficult to defend, especially against attack by undermining, and in later versions of the keepless castle, such as Conway in North Wales, the corner towers were kept more in line with the general perimeter. An intermediate step towards the keepless castle can be seen at Helmsley, where the keep is placed in the outer wall.

Katherine Parr, sixth and last wife of Henry VIII, lived at the castle. Born at Kendal she married Henry in 1543. Before that she was married twice, the second time to one of the Danby Latimers. A story persists that Henry once visited her at the castle, sheltering during a gale at a farm ever since called Stormy Hall. But the farm's name is probably derived from a family named Esturmi who occupied the house for a long period from the thirteenth century.

The most impressive internal feature of the castle is the banqueting room. With its huge stone fireplace this is generally called the Courtroom, for each October it houses the annual sitting of the Danby Court Leet, one of several ancient manor courts surviving in the North York Moors.

The Danby Court dates from 1656 when five joint landowners sold the Danby estate to an ancestor of the present owner, Viscount Downe. For many years the deed of sale was kept at Danby vicarage, in a chest that could be opened only by five keys.

The court's job is to administer the common rights over the 11,000-acre estate. A solicitor acts as clerk or steward, with 13 jurymen representing more than 100 people with common rights on the moors. The jury makes an annual tour of inspection. It deals with matters ranging from applications for moor grazing or peat cutting to plans for laying drains across the moor, or constructing a road or garage. In 1971 the neighbouring manor court of Spaunton, with jurisdiction over 7,000 acres, published its first decimalised table of tariffs. The annual payment for a cottage garden on manorial land was fixed at 50p. For a hay-shed the charge was £1, for a joiner's shop 30p, for a manure heap 50p, and for a milk-stand 10p. The court sits once a year, in the living room of Manor House Farm, home of the jury foreman, Mr Thomas Strickland.

Spanning the River Esk at the foot of a lane running from Danby Castle is the narrow hump-backed Duck Bridge. Like the castle, this carries the Neville coat-of-arms, retained when the bridge was rebuilt in the eighteenth century by a mason named George Duck, from whom it takes its name. With its parapet now incredibly gouged by cars, the bridge was probably built originally at about the same time as the castle. It is said to have been one of three erected on the orders of three sisters, Lucia, Margaret and Catherine de Thweng, whose family owned the Danby estate until it passed by marriage to the Latimers. The other two bridges have vanished, but a fragment of one can be seen upstream of the present river bridge at Danby's neighbouring village of Castleton.

As its name suggests, Castleton also had a castle. The road between the village and the railway station runs along the ditch

116

that divided the inner and outer defences: on the east, the site of the keep is occupied for a farmhouse, while to the west a former Methodist chapel crowns the outer bank. Believed to have been built about 1135, the castle was probably the first in the district, destined to be replaced by Danby when William Latimer took over the estate. It is unlikely that the castle ever consisted of more than wooden buildings protected by a timber palisade.

By the Esk near Castleton's cricket field stands a former mill, converted into houses in the mid-1970s. The building is a link with an almost forgotten industry of North Yorkshire—weaving. Flax from the Baltic region was spun into cloth at the mill, which opened in the late eighteenth century. Then it employed thirty people, among them girls only nine years old. The finished cloth was made into clothes and other items by local cottage weavers. The success of the enterprise led to a general market being established at Castleton, but competition from steam eventually put the mill out of business. It was adapted for grinding corn, and before World War II it served as a blacksmith's shop.

A more specialised market once thrived at the hamlet of Houlsyke, a short distance west of Danby. In the days when Britain was self-sufficient in meat, Eskdale became a notable pig-rearing area. Salting and curing took place at Houlsyke, where dealers also gathered. Horse-drawn wagons carried the district's produce, which included lamb, mutton and wool as well as bacon and pork, down to Whitby, from where much of it was shipped to London. One dealer in the capital had a weekly order for forty sheep carcases. In Houlsyke most of the trading took place in a pub known as the Fat Ox, now a house.

Another village of the Danby district is Westerdale. Besides its unusual Bulmer Stone (see p 112), it features an ancient packhorse bridge. Known as Hunter's Sty it displays the Duncombe coronet and a tablet recording its (heavy-handed) restoration in 1874. Nearby is a former Victorian shooting lodge of the Duncombe's, converted to a youth hostel in 1947.

Westerdale continues to attract visitors looking for the former home of Major J. Fairfax-Blakeborough. Until he died in 1976, aged ninety-two, this remarkable man contributed a column on country topics to many northern newspapers. Published in some of these papers for more than fifty years, this column was largely responsible for making the major a legend in his own lifetime. He also wrote more than 100 books, mostly on rural life and sport, particularly horse-racing. But Low House, the major's old home in Westerdale parish, is a full 2 miles from the village, actually nearer Castleton. As a young man the major lived at Battersby Old Hall, where an oak tree, planted by the major in 1973 to mark his ninetieth birthday, can be seen by the roadside.

Undoubtedly the most remarkable venture in the Danby district is the community for mentally handicapped people centred on Botton Hall. Established in 1955 by the Camphill Village Trust, which has since set up 3 similar communities in Britain and 13 abroad, the project began with a handful of handicapped people working a 250-acre farm. Today, the community extends to 4 farms covering more than 400 acres, plus numerous workshops in which high-quality craft goods are made. With its own church and social centre, and a tiny village square complete with post office, gift shop, book shop and coffee bar, Botton is well worth a visit. A useful way of life is being provided for about 133 'villagers', who are aided in running their largely self-sufficient way of life by about 70 staff or co-workers.

The name Camphill, incidentally, comes from a house in Aberdeen in which the founders of the movement started a school for mentally handicapped children in 1939. In 1976 Danby figured in a significant advance in the trust's work when it became linked with a new 'satellite' home at Old Malton: one of only three in England, it provides residential accommodation for mentally handicapped people who are considered capable of working in the general community.

For many people an introduction to the varied attractions of the Danby district comes in the National Park Centre, opened in 1975 in Danby Lodge by the North York Moors National Park Committee. The use of this former shooting lodge as a

Plates 12 and 13 Time off: *(above)* the original Sun Inn or Spout House (left) and its 1914 replacement. Of cruck construction, the thatched 'Spout' is one of the oldest buildings in the national park; *(below)* Sleddale Beck near Kildale, typical of many similar places that are today popular among picnickers

Plate 14 Hawnby — romantic scenery of a kind not usually associated with the moors. But although Ryedale is rich in such scenes, immediately beyond the hill lies one of the wildest and least visited tracts of moorland, centred on Snilesworth

place where visitors can learn about the moors echoes a comment made more than a century ago by the Cleveland historian Ord, who spoke of parties setting forth from the lodge to 'explore the wild mountainous scenery of the neighbourhood'.

Once on display in the lodge was a Golden Eagle, shot at Staingate in December 1807. This was not the last eagle in the North York Moors, for Canon Atkinson reports that the bird was still sometimes seen during his early days at Danby in the middle of the nineteenth century. On one memorable day, the canon saw an eagle, a pair of hen-harriers, and a 'large-hawk', probably a buzzard, all on the same moor. 'Once I have seen the kite here, and in the older days ravens used to breed and might be seen or heard any day,' he observes.

In recent years, buzzards have returned to breed in the moors, hen-harriers have been seen, and in 1974 a dead kite was found in Bilsdale. But no ravens have been sighted, and it seems unlikely that a Golden Eagle will ever again swoop over the fine moor-and-dale scenery around Danby.

Mulgrave Woods

On Wednesdays and at weekends, Lord Normanby opens his woods at Mulgrave Castle to the public—free of charge. This pleasant tradition, which began long before the present marquis was born, gives visitors to the North York Moors a chance to enjoy an outing-with-a-difference. Excluding Forestry Commission plantations, large areas of woodland, especially the old English kind, are not common in the moors. Those around Mulgrave Castle are probably the most extensive in the district.

The responsibility for landscaping the estate belongs largely to William Repton whose book of plans, dated 1792, is kept at the castle. An interesting feature of the work was the laying out of a section of the garden as an artificial battery, pleasingly called the Quarter Deck. Writing in the 1840s, the local historian John Walker Ord described the view from there as the finest conceivable, comprising the calm unruffled azure of the German Ocean, the venerable ruins of Whitby Abbey, the pier and ships entering the harbour, a distant peep of the hermitage and the old castle, with the far hills and moors beyond.

Charles Dickens, who stayed at the castle in 1844, was reportedly in such ecstasy with this same scene that he literally danced on the velvet-smooth greensward of the Quarter Deck.

Although public access does not normally extend to the Quarter Deck, there are plenty of places where the qualities apparent to Dickens and Ord can still be felt. The various features of the woods need to be described with some care, for there are three castles—or rather two and the site of a third.

Mulgrave Castle, the ancestral home, is really a country house. The core of the building is Georgian, built some time shortly before 1735 for the Duchess of Buckingham, a daughter of James II and wife of the Earl of Mulgrave. Two wings, also Georgian, were added in the 1780s. From about 1805 to 1816 an architect named William Atkinson completed the castle fantasy, with towers, turrets and further battlements, as well as a projecting entrance hall.

Besides Dickens, William Wordsworth was a guest at the castle. During or just before one visit he wrote:

> I have been to Whitby several times; once in particular I remember seeing a most extraordinary effect from the pier, produced by the bold and ragged shore in a misty and showery day. The appearance was as of a set of huge faces in profile, one behind the other, with noses of prodigious prominence; the whole was very fantastic and yet grand.

On a clear day this striking view can still be seen, especially from Whitby's west pier.

Mulgrave woods clothe the sides of two narrow valleys that reach the sea at Sandsend within a few hundred yards of each other. About half a mile inland, on the ridge dividing the valleys, are the overgrown ruins of a Norman castle—the one referred to by Ord. The keep is of particular interest. It was modified to meet a defect common to most keeps, in which the square corners created dead angles, allowing attackers to work at the foot. The Mulgrave keep was modified by the addition of round towers, grafted on to the rectangular corners. According to some experts this adaptation is unique in England.

Mulgrave castle is believed to have been started in about 1200 by Robert Turnham, an armour-bearer to Richard I. In 1214 it was acquired by a Frenchman named Peter de Mauley, who married Turnham's daughter. It is sometimes said that local people, regarding the castle as a burden, changed the district's named from Moultgrace (much beauty) to Multgrave (much oppression). The most likely derivation of Mulgrave, however, is from 'Muli', a personal name, and 'grif', a steep-sided valley. In 1614 the castle was dismantled by order of Parliament, but there is evidence that part of it was occupied until early in the nineteenth century.

Half a mile to the north-west is the mound of an earlier castle. In the eleventh and twelfth centuries the mound was probably surmounted by a wooden building; some people believe that the mound itself may date back to Roman times, and may have been connected with the Roman Road (see p 76).

The hermitage mentioned by Ord is now a ruined summer-house. There is a belief that it stands on the site of a temple to Thor—a claim linked with the fact that East Row, part of Sandsend, was once called Thordisa after the pagan god. The hermitage may also have been attached for a time to Whitby Abbey, for a charter of 1150 notes the setting up of a cell in this vicinity, with an order that 'divine service be daily celebrated by some priest of Whitby'.

In recent years, Mulgrave's deciduous woods have been intermixed with small conifer plantations, but in due season the woods still abound with snowdrops, bluebells and other wild flowers. And while there are a few other woods of equal, or perhaps greater, beauty in the North York Moors—notably at Sinnington, Glaisdale, Rievaulx and Littlebeck—none has the romantic trappings of Mulgrave. Around the back of the Hermitage, a track leads to the Wizard's Glen, a recess graced by a 24ft waterfall. Elsewhere, part of the main public path, which is most easily followed from the East Row car park, runs through a rock tunnel, a delight for children. Between the Norman castle and Lord Normanby's home there is a chasm known as the Footman's leap, where a love-sick servant supposedly jumped to his death.

7

THE AGE OF THE RAILWAY

Rosedale

Few enterprises in the North York Moors stir the imagination as much as the Rosedale Railway. It is not hard to see why. The line leaps with sensational suddenness from the plain of Cleveland. Near Ingleby Greenhow it scales the escarpment by an incline almost a mile long. With the gradient stiffening from 1–11 through 1–8 to 1–5, the track stands out boldly from many miles to the north, as though engraved on the hillside against a giant ruler.

From the top of the incline, the line runs for 11 miles across the roof of the moors. Probably no other standard-gauge railway in England operated in a more unlikely setting. Skilfully engineered virtually to eliminate the need for expensive bridges, the line swings in long loops round the valley heads, never once dropping below 1,000ft. The views from the track, first into Farndale and then 'Rosedale, are superb. And the line's termination at Bank Top, Rosedale, is almost as dramatic as Ingleby Incline—an abrupt halt where the local moorland road takes a 1–3 plunge to the valley.

The wild situation of many of the cottages built to serve the line is also impressive. A group of three at Incline Top was known as 'Siberia'. Two more cottages stood at Blowith, where the line crosses Rudland Rigg, near the highest point of the moors. By happy chance, Blowith even sounds like an engine in steam; and as you stand there it is easy to picture the ponderous goods trains clanking along, the waved greetings from cab to cottage, the departing brake van, and the silence surging back across the moors. This is the magic of the Rosedale Railway.

The line owes its creation to the Victorian exploitation of Rosedale's iron ore, beginning in 1856. At first the ore was hauled by horse and cart to Pickering Station, but in 1857 the North Eastern Railway began a series of surveys that led to the opening of the 14-mile Rosedale branch on 27 March 1861. At its northern end the line joined the existing network at Battersby, 2 miles beyond the foot of the incline. From there the ore went via Stokesley station to Ferryhill or Stockton, not to Middlesbrough via Great Ayton as is widely supposed.

To reach the foot of the incline, where former railway cottages remain occupied as homes, the NER extended and widened a narrow-gauge line already laid to a mine on Ingleby Bank. Some of the masonry of this mine can be seen from a forestry road due south of Bank Foot Farm. Particularly interesting are a number of grooved boulders, probably laid between the rails of a tramway used for hauling tubs, to prevent the iron rope fouling the ground.

Locomotives working the new line could not operate up and down the incline. They were therefore stationed at Bank Top, Rosedale. The sharp angles at the bottom and top of the incline meant that when a locomotive needed to be lowered for major repairs, the central pair of its three sets of wheels had to be removed—a task normally carried out at Rosedale.

Although most of the branch was single track, part of the incline was double with a third track at the very top. Fully laden trucks, descending 3 at a time, provided the power for hauling up the empty wagons. This normally took about 3 minutes at 20mph. A continuous cable, 1,650yd long, passed over 2 drums in a tall drum house, with 1 drum paying out the cable as the other reeled it in. The base of the drum house still stands, and until 1974 there was also the empty shell of the last surviving Incline Top cottage—an evocative ruin that it was sad to see destroyed.

As a precaution against trucks running away on the incline, an iron snag protruded between the rails of the up track. This jammed against the axle if the trucks rolled back. A similar snag was provided on the down track, lifted into action when needed by a lever. An additional safety measure to prevent trucks rolling back was a slight hump in the track just beyond the summit of the incline. Each ascending set of wagons also triggered off a bell, so that the brakeman, in charge of the drum house, could pinpoint its position in fog or darkness.

A second incline, half a mile long, ran between Rosedale Bank Top and a drift mine at Hollins—the first mine to be developed. Narrow-gauge tubs were hauled up this incline by steam power from a stationary boiler. The 100ft Rosedale Chimney, part of the boiler house, was a celebrated moorland landmark until it was demolished in July 1972—another regrettable loss. The chimney's builder, John Flintoft, is said to have danced a jig on the top when it was completed in 1861.

Still prominent at Bank Top is a row of kilns, into which ore was tipped to be calcined, or roasted. This lowered the moisture content and the weight of the ore, thereby reducing the royalties payable to the landowner.

Two sets of kilns, an early bank of 16 and a later one of 3, survive on the Rosedale East branch. $4\frac{3}{4}$ miles long, this branch diverges from the main Rosedale Railway at Blakey Ridge. There, the builders constructed the only bridge of the entire network, since demolished. The branch runs round the head of Rosedale to its terminus at Low Baring. Nearby is a second chimney, which was a mine ventilation shaft. The goods shed is now a farm building and the agent's house a whitewashed cottage. In the 1870s a narrow-gauge tramway served mines beyond the limit of the line. It was worked by two engines named Rosedale and Emily, and its route can still be picked out.

At Bank Top the Hollins drift incline can be identified by a blocked-up archway where the track passed underneath the moorland road. Soon after the branch opened, there was a dramatic accident when a coupling snapped and several tubs careered down the line. A contemporary report said: 'The whole lot were seen rushing downwards with fearful rapidity, illuminating the line with fire which in the darkness was truly awful.' We can imagine the awesome scenes when similar accidents occurred on the Ingleby Incline—despite the precautions.

Even when the Hollins mine closed, Bank Top continued to be the railway headquarters. The engine shed, which housed up to five engines, was ultimately demolished in 1937–8, the stone being used to build Hutton-le-Hole's village hall. The shed's foundations still remain, together with filled-in inspection pits and sixteen deserted cottages: even their taps bore the initials NER.

In its lifetime the railway supplied 10 million tons of ore to the North-East iron and steel industry. The peak year was 1873 when, with all 4 of the mines served by the branch in operation (see pp 53 and 103) 560,668 tons were carried—over 1,500 tons per day. Trains of up to 15 trucks shuttled to and fro across the moors, with 6 trains per day arriving at Incline Foot from Stockton or Ferryhill to collect the ore.

Successive mine closures led to a sharp decline, and the final annual output, before the end of all mining in 1926, was just 14,000 tons—less than a fortnight's production in the heyday. The railway remained busy for a few more years, transporting calcined dust to Teesside. When the last load went down Ingleby Incline on 11 January 1929, work on lifting the track began immediately. The line's last spectacle was a massive improvised jacking operation at Incline Top, to remove the centre wheels of the track-lifting loco. And when this engine was lowered down the incline on 8 June 1929, the Rosedale Railway was no more.

Throughout the line's history a tremendous battle had been waged against the weather. During the construction period 40 navvies were trapped at Esklets, sheltering in a cottage that became completely covered by snow. In 1882–3 the line was blocked from 2 December until February, and in 1894–5 it was closed from December until mid-April. The latter winter was so severe that 200 hapless grouse took shelter in Lastingham. Snow lingered in cuttings on the Rosedale Railway until June, and a strip of black snow was discovered under a pile of iron-stone in mid-August.

The NER built special snowploughs for the line, some includ-ing a cab with sleeping quarters and a stove. But the snow was often so deep that the workmen simply became imprisoned in the machines. In 1916–17, with drifts up to 30ft deep, it took 75 men 3 days to clear 1 cutting. And at the end of the line's life the weather played a wry joke, freezing the whistle of the track-lifting loco!

But for all the hardship, the line won the affection of many of the people who ran it. Several railwaymen returned to the branch after leaving it. Among them was Jacob Baker who spent fifty-one years on the Rosedale Railway. He was once fined for 'slow running', an offence perhaps connected with his known fondness for stopping to catch game.

The isolated cottagers developed a strong community spirit. Children on the moor top went by train to school in Farndale. Groceries came along the line from either Great Broughton, near Stokesley, or Rosedale. The orders were usually pooled in a single wagon load, and at Blakey a weekly gathering of cotta-gers met the train and sorted out their own provisions.

Railway workmen and their families were allowed to travel in the brake vans—a facility they used for shopping trips to Middlesbrough or Stockton. The cottagers also enjoyed fre-quent get-togethers. Mrs P. E. Longster of Darlington, whose grandparents lived in the crossing house, which she said bore an enamel nameplate and was demolished in World War II, wrote to me in 1972 with her memories of Blowith.

My grandparents always kept a pig and hens, and in winter a brush and shovel to dig a way to the well, which was across the line. A flagpole marked the spot, which many a time was covered by snow. At Christmas we all met at Mr. Joseph Featherstone's [Incline Top], also the Farndale Singers. My granny was never lonely, although there would be days when she would see only the trains pass by, and she was very sad to leave that cosy old stone house.

The well mentioned by Mrs Longster is still there, and my hands have become numb with cold clearing out the rubble that accumulates in it. My souvenirs of the Rosedale Railway include a length of the Ingleby Incline cable, a railway trackseat, and a fine poem in dialect, sent to me anonymously with an excellent pen-and-ink drawing of the Rosedale Chimney. The railway has many friends, aware of the echoes that this tremendous venture still sends around the moors.

Paddy Waddell

By Liverton Lane End on the Whitby–Guisborough moor road lie the prominent remains of a railway that never was. Two sections of embankment punctuate the moor to the south while a shallow cutting runs away to the north. The name of the railway that these lonely features were intended to serve has a curious, even rather comic ring—the Paddy Waddell Railway.

The name is easily explained. Paddy Waddell was John Waddell, a civil engineering contractor from Edinburgh. His firm built Putney Bridge, the Mersey Rail Tunnel and the approaches to the Tay Bridge. The first engine to cross the ill-fated Tay Bridge was later used by Waddell in the construction of the Whitby–Scarborough Railway. Waddell completed that line in the 1880s soon after building its northern counterpart, the Whitby–Loftus coastal railway. But Waddell's name has stuck to the abortive venture symbolised by the Liverton Lane earthworks and one or two other forlorn fragments in the moors.

In January 1872 the *Whitby Gazette* published the first news of this luckless enterprise. 'In addition to the lines already in operation and in course of formation in the Cleveland district, a new line is projected, still further to open out the great mineral wealth of the country,' it reported. The idea was to supply ironstone from the main Cleveland field, in the Skelton–Brotton area, to ironworks that had opened in Glaisdale in 1866.

Properly known as the Cleveland Mineral Extension Railway, the line would diverge from the coastal system at Lingdale and join the NER's Esk Valley line west of Glaisdale—a distance of 10½ miles.

The railway was proposed by Mr Joseph Dodds, a Winston (Barnard Castle) man who became MP for Stockton. Subscribers included Lord Downe and C. F. Bolckow, son of the Teesside ironfounder. But the first attempt to obtain parliamentary approval was blocked by opposition from the Whitby, Redcar and Middlesbrough Railway, then busy promoting the Whitby–Loftus line. A bill finally received royal assent in July 1873, but this proved to be only the start of a long chapter of misfortunes.

With few investors coming forward, the period allowed under the act for constructing the line ran out. In 1878 a 're-vival' act had to be obtained, followed by a second revival act in 1881. In all, Parliament passed seven acts authorising the construction of the line. But although these acts spanned almost a quarter of a century, from 1873 until the 1896 deadline of the last act, the line was never built!

Work started and stopped many times. On 17 October 1874, an official turf-cutting ceremony was performed at Moorsholm by Joseph Dodds. The *Whitby Gazette*'s report described the setting as a 'remote, bleak and at this season almost inaccessible part of the district'. But despite these uncomplimentary words Moorsholm soon blossomed with a railway hotel—one that never opened for business. Containing seven bedrooms and a spacious reception hall, the gaunt building still stands, hugely out of scale with the rest of the village. When I visited it in 1974 I found it to be occupied by Miss Elizabeth Marsay, daughter of the man who built it. The furnishings were virtually unchanged from Victorian times. The reception hall included a hatch, for serving drinks to travellers who never arrived. Nearby was a row of bells, to summon servants who were never employed. Even the original switches for the bells were still in place in the principal rooms, scarcely ever handled in earnest since the day they were installed. Miss Marsay told me she believed that

131

Paddy Waddell's chief engineer lodged with her father, possibly qualifying as the hotel's only guest.

Another interesting reminder of the line exists at Woodhall Bridge, where the Lealholm–Ugthorpe road crosses Stonegate Beck. There the promoters wished to build a level crossing. Local people agreed, on condition that a passenger station was included. The station was never built, but the incongruous iron bridge spanning the stream marks the beginning of an embankment that was to have formed one of the approaches to the station. An uncompleted cutting, also visible, was to have served the same purpose on the other side of the line.

Two buildings became inns during the construction period. These were Rake House, a distinctive farmhouse near Glaisdale, and the Laughing Ass, now a modernised cottage by the Lealholm–Stonegate road. In front of Rake House is the line's only other bridge, carrying a farm road over the bed of the Paddy Waddell Railway, which joins the Esk Valley line near this point. As in its railway-navvy days, Rake House still burns peat. The occupier also pays a traditional sixpenny tithe for grazing rights to the local Court Leet—a link with another aspect of moorland history. The beams of the house are said to have been made of ships' timbers from Whitby.

Three circumstances led to the failure of the Paddy Waddell project. With the great railway boom already fading when the scheme was launched, confidence was hard to generate. The closure of the Glaisdale ironworks in 1876 added to the difficulties, and as the whole of the iron trade slipped into a deep depression in the 1880s all hope of the new railway attracting adequate support virtually vanished. Boldly—or perhaps desperately—inaugurating physical work in 1882, the directors pointed in vain to the 160 million tons of ironstone estimated to lie alongside the line between Lingdale and the Whitby Moor road. One of the last places where work seems to have taken place was in a cutting north of Stonegate Mill, where many loose boulders are strewn about.

John Waddell was probably nicknamed Paddy from the number of Irishmen employed on his schemes. But his family was grand enough to have its own crest. Nine years after Paddy's death in 1888 his firm was still trying to salvage something from the wreck of the Cleveland Mineral Extension Railway. In particular it campaigned for the parliamentary deposit of £8,000 to be divided among the creditors. Paddy Waddell himself seems to have possessed a Scot's dour sense of humour, for when it was publicly stated that the Whitby–Scarborough line was lucky to have such a good contractor, he glumly replied that he was not so fortunate to find a good employer. His comments about the railway that now bears his name must have been unprintable.

Whitby–Pickering

In 1965 the Whitby–Pickering Railway apparently perished under the Beeching axe. But on a sunny May day in 1973 the Duchess of Kent reopened the line as the North Yorkshire Moors Railway. Bells rang out in Whitby, and at Grosmont sightseers almost blocked the line as the Duchess boarded a ceremonial train to Pickering. The *Whitby Gazette* summed up the happy occasion:

> The countryside through which the railway winds its way has never looked lovelier. One of the biggest trackside crowds was at that favourite picnic area Moorgates where the line passes under the Goathland to Pickering road. At isolated Darnholm a Union Jack was stuck in the bankside, and the entire family of a single house at lonely Farwath turned out to wave to the Duchess . . . . If Whitby was charmed with the attractive petite Duchess, so was Pickering where the crowds seemed even larger than at Whitby . . .

This was not very different from the orginal opening of 1836 when a report noted that

> every part of the line where the public could have access to it, or where a view of the railway could be obtained was crowded with spectators . . . Many flags were exhibited and the most hearty cheers were given and returned by the bystanders and those in the coaches.

133

On that occasion five bands played at Pickering, where 7,000 people turned out. And when the revellers returned to Whitby they celebrated at the Angel Inn from 5pm to 2am.

High feeling seems inseparable from the Whitby–Pickering Railway. When the line faced closure its supporters put up one of the country's staunchest fights to try and keep it alive. When restoration was proposed so much help was offered that by opening day the line boasted a preservation society with 9,000 members—the largest railway group of its kind in Britain. The enthusiasts had succeeded in restoring the longest stretch of standard-gauge railway (18 miles) then in the care of a voluntary group.

All this underlines the teeming history of the line. Its surveyor was George Stephenson, who came to it fresh from his triumphs with the Stockton and Darlington Railway and the Liverpool–Manchester Railway. Charles Dickens was once a passenger on the line, which he described as 'a quaint old railway along part of which passengers are hauled by a rope'—a reference to a 500yd incline at Beck Hole.

In 1864 special locomotives, nicknamed Whitby bogies, were built for the line. To cope with the exceptionally sharp curves of the track, their 2 pairs of bogie wheels were placed closer together than usual and set farther back under the boiler. Special coaches were also developed for the line. With 4 wheels instead of the usual 6 they became known as the Whitby Bathing Machines. Some ran direct to and from King's Cross, and W. A. Tuplin, a railway historian, has indicated their standard of comfort by observing that 'any passenger who travelled in one at high Great Northern speed from York to London might feel he needed another holiday immediately'.

The railway gave the world what is claimed to have been the first cheap-day excursion. For a fete at Grosmont in 1839, to raise money for a new Anglican church, the return fare from Whitby was reduced from 9d (4½p) to 6d (2½p), with corresponding reductions from Pickering. The church was completed in 1842 but soon became inadequate as

Grosmont's population increased during the local ironstone boom. When the building was replaced by the present church in 1875, its east window was carefully transferred to the same position in the new church. It had been commissioned originally as a memorial to Henry Belcher, a Whitby solicitor who organised the historic fete. He also wrote a pioneer study of the Whitby–Pickering railway.

A 6-mile section of the railway, between Whitby and Grosmont, escaped closure in 1965. Used by trains operating British Rail's Esk Valley service, this is not part of the North Yorkshire Moors Railway, which nevertheless covers the much greater distance between Grosmont and Pickering. The train journey takes the visitor through the impressive gorge of Newton Dale, a trip that cannot be done by car. Today the still silent landscape is perhaps too much dominated by forestry, but there are still large areas of bracken and crag, where the grandeur of the dale, with its towering cliffs, is fully felt. The dale once contained farmhouses that must have been among the loneliest in Yorkshire. One stood below a large rock with a hole in it, just visible through trees from the train. An Eskdale farmer used to say that before the railway came his mother was 'born at t'Needle's Eye'. He told friends: 'If they lost their fire they went wi t'warming pan ti t'neighbours en gat a bit o'live fire en carried it heame ti start afresh.'

The railway was promoted as a goods line. Materials transported in the early years included Grosmont ironstone, shipped from Whitby to Tyneside. Esk Valley whinstone also went via the railway to the port, some ending up in famous buildings such as Somerset House and Waterloo Bridge.

At first the line was a horse-tramway, and it was because Stephenson had engineered the line with only the horse in mind that the Whitby bogies were needed. At Grosmont the original stable block can be seen, while today's engine shed, open to visitors, is reached through the narrow castellated tunnel used by the horse-drawn trains. A small building next to the present Station Hotel was once the Tunnel Inn, and down in Newton Dale a house called the Grange, now a field centre, was formerly the Raindale Inn—a changing post for the horses.

The most notable feature of the horse-worked line was the incline mentioned by Dickens. He travelled on the railway in 1844 to attend a friend's funeral in Malton, having stayed over-night at Mulgrave Castle. The carriages were uncoupled at the incline and a tank of water was released down the slope to haul them up. This system continued even when steam trains were introduced in 1846, but a 4-mile deviation, eliminating the incline, was opened in 1865. Today the abandoned track is available to walkers over most of its length, and the incline forms part of a particularly attractive stretch, between Goathland and Grosmont. The simple walk between these places, calling at the beautiful village of Beck Hole, can be conveniently combined with a ride in the opposite direction on a Moors Railway steam train.

The introduction of steam and the improvements to the track were due to George Hudson, immortalised as the Railway King through the number of schemes he promoted and controlled. It is also to Hudson, who acquired the Whitby–Pickering railway in 1845, that Whitby owes its development as a resort. Having linked the line for the first time to the wider rail network, Hudson bought Whitby West Fields, now the West Cliff. He arranged for the building of the Royal Hotel and the cliff road known as the Khyber Pass. When Hudson's empire collapsed in 1849 amid claims of embezzlement, Hudson's work at Whitby was continued by Sir George Elliot, a former Durham pit boy. Elliot built the Spa and is said to have lived in a house at the seaward end of Whitby's Crescent.

This century, the name to be written large in the history of the Whitby–Pickering railway is Tom Salmon, of Ruswarp. It was he who decided in 1967 that this famous railway should not die, although to many people it already seemed well and truly dead. Mr Salmon and a handful of supporters, many of them railwaymen or ex-railwaymen, formed a pilot group. For a time they were derided as 'the Crackpots', but the railway that they and their growing band of followers saved is now one of Yorkshire's most popular attractions. Together with George

Stephenson, George Hudson and Charles Dickens, Tom Salmon, the local man, is worth a thought in any ride on the moorland railway.

The Esk Valley

To many people it might seem incredible that the world of the country railway, with local trains shuffling on their timeless journeys between peaceful village stations, survives in the North York Moors. But so it does: British Rail's Esk Valley Line is an idyll from a vanished age—the perfect picture of branch-line England.

If the Whitby–Pickering Railway is notable for its grandeur, the Esk Valley Line is unequalled for charm. Regular users are confident it is the country's most beautiful train ride. I agree with them and do not find it hard to say why. For 28 miles the line runs within the national park. It calls at eleven moorland stations, with glimpses of church towers and pantiled roofs among the trees. It is on intimate terms with celebrated features of the moors such as Roseberry Topping, Captain Cook's Monument, and the Beggar's Bridge, Glaisdale. And for most of its length it is never far from the meandering Esk, Yorkshire's only salmon river and centrepiece of some of the county's finest scenery.

How strange, therefore, that the line is so little praised. A popular book on the Whitby–Pickering Railway dismisses it as 'the straggling branch to Battersby'. A few years ago an article appeared in a Yorkshire newspaper expressing surprise that the line existed at all. Not until 1973 did British Rail launch a much overdue publicity campaign for the railway, which it re-named the Esk Valley Line. Until then it was merely the Middlesbrough–Whitby service—not a description likely to induce a box-office stampede.

One reason why the line has attracted so little attention is that unlike the Whitby–Pickering Railway it was not developed to a single overall design. It is a railway of bits and pieces. Promoted by the North Yorkshire and Cleveland Railway Company, it was essentially a speculative offshoot from the main line between Northallerton and Stockton, itself part of the Leeds–Northern network.

The railway diverged from the main line at Picton, south of Yarm. The tentative nature of the scheme is indicated by advice from the company engineer that the line should not be taken beyond Stokesley unless ironstone traffic could be obtained, presumably from Grosmont. The directors must have become satisfied on this, for when the line reached Stokesley in 1857, work promptly began on an extension to Battersby, engineered by Robert Stephenson, son of George. From there the line was extended to Castleton (1861) and Grosmont (1865). The track of the Whitby–Pickering Railway could then be used for the remainder of the route to Whitby.

Meanwhile, under separate legislation, a spur was added northwards from Battersby. By joining the Middlesbrough–Guisborough Railway near Nunthorpe this spur gave the Esk Valley Line a link with the principal Teesside town of Middlesbrough. A tangled web indeed!

But despite this patchwork background, the railway has a definite unity. Indeed, the Whitby–Grosmont section, with 10 crossings of the Esk in 6 miles, seems more akin to the rest of the Esk Valley Line than to the Whitby–Pickering Railway for which it was built!

Although no dramatic difficulties were encountered in constructing the line, an unusual problem arose near Danby. Rail travellers will notice that the cuttings are wider than usual, with their bank-sides more gently graded. These adaptations became necessary because of slippage of the moorland clays and shales during the construction period, compelling the workmen to remake the cuttings several times. Asked his opinion of the local countryside, the resident engineer retorted: 'Why sir, it is the devil of a countryside.'

An interesting aspect of the line's history is that initially it did not link Whitby with Middlesbrough, as it does now, for the original Teesside terminus was Stockton. Even when the first passenger trains were introduced from Middlesbrough, they went via Stockton, thus starting their journey to the Yorkshire coast by running into Durham!

Eventually, one or two Middlesbrough trains ran direct to the Esk Valley, via Great Ayton. This involved reversing from Battersby, which until then had been simply a station on the through line from Stockton. The reversal of all trains, a curious feature of the line's operation today, became unavoidable when the Battersby–Picton section closed in 1954.

Between 1857 and 1892 the Battersby–Picton section had its own branch—a 2-mile mineral railway running to ironstone mines in Scugdale. This line's fortunes, like those of the mines, probably declined sharply after 1888 when a large migration of miners took place from Scugdale to Rosedale.

In the Esk Valley itself, a mineral railway served brickworks at Commondale. Until the mid-1950s, a tank locomotive stood among the ruins of the brickyard, since cleared to make way for a Scout camp. Other remains of the railway, mostly bridge abutments and embankments, can still be seen.

When the coastal railway north of Whitby closed in 1958, the Esk Valley Line became the only rail route between Whitby and Teesside. This brought a considerable increase in traffic, with 29 passenger trains on the line each day, 15 more than in the 'golden age' at the turn of the century. Even in more recent times, the line has enjoyed a fuller basic service than on its completion in 1865—about 6 trains each way per day, compared with only 4.

For some older people the line has a unique memory, recalled by the late George Harland of Glaisdale, in his valuable booklet of reminiscences, *Queen of the Dales*. During a lantern-slide lecture given by a Hartlepool doctor, a short piece of film was screened, showing a train entering Grosmont station. 'When we saw this it nearly took our breath away,' says Mr Harland. 'But this was nothing to the surprise when a Glaisdale youth was seen walking down the platform. This was our first time seeing a moving picture.'

In common with the Whitby–Pickering Railway, the Esk Valley Line was threatened with closure in 1965. The success of the campaign to retain the line reflects the railway's importance to the communities of the Esk Valley, many of which are without a bus service. Local pride in the line led a year or two ago to the formation of the Esk Valley Line Committee—a group of friends of the railway, dedicated to improving the service and stimulating interest in it; the group even has plans to revive the much lamented Best Kept Station competition. British Rail's own promotion sensibly emphasises the line's advantages to walkers, for whom the succession of stations opens up a wide range of possibilities.

It is sad that for many people the appeal of railways apparently still begins and ends with steam. To me, the sight of the Esk Valley's neat diesel units, clattering by the Esk or waiting patiently at some village station, always brings great pleasure. Even the sound of the klaxon or the distant rattle of the wheels is good to hear—evidence of the living railway of the moors.

When I was waiting to board a train at Battersby one day in 1976, time might well have slipped back fifty years, for the station garden was bright with flowers and a handwritten notice announced that messages for tickets for an excursion could be left at the signal box. During deep snow the following winter, I found the platform obligingly swept and a blazing store-room fire before which I and my fellow passengers chatted as we kept warm.

And if you peep into the disused water tank on Battersby platform, you will see a fine shoal of goldfish—successors to a well loved pair put in by a railwayman long ago. With an effort of imagination, a restored railway might create such an eccentric attraction, but on the old rural branch-lines such things just happened.

8

HERE'S A CHURCH . . .

St Gregory's Minster

People who expect a minster to be a cathedral or at least a large church are surprised when they come across St Gregory's Minster—that is, if they come across it at all. Half-hidden among trees, the tiny parish church might escape the notice even of those who follow the special signposts to it from the road between Helmsley and Kirbymoorside.

In its beautiful setting near the famous Kirkdale Cave (see p 16), the church is a place of absorbing interest. The best pointer to its great wealth of history is the Saxon sundial carved on a 7ft slab of stone above the south doorway. The most complete example of its kind in the world, and now protected from the weather by a nineteenth-century porch, it bears an inscription that is worth much more than a passing glance. In the vernacular spelling of the period it explains how Orm, son of Gamal, 'bohte' (bought) St Gregory's Minster when it was 'all tobrocan and to falan', and had it 'made anew from the grund', to Christ and St Gregory, in the days of Edward the King and Tosti, Earl of Northumberland.

The untidy arrangement of the lines and words suggests that the inscription was not properly worked out before the mason began his work. Nevertheless, it tells us far more than its author can ever have imagined. There is great significance, for instance, in the revelation that a 'minster', or mission house existed at St Gregory's before the rebuilding of the monastery by Orm, centuries before the founding of the great monastic houses of Fountains, Rievaulx, Byland and the rest.

The reference to Tosti enables a close estimate to be made of the date when the mission station was replaced by the present church. This must have been between 1055 and 1065, respectively the years when Tosti became Earl of Northumberland and when he was defeated by King Harold at Stamford Bridge.

By noting that Orme 'bohte' St Gregory's Minster, the sundial touches on the ancient practice by which many churches became part of the patronage of a local lord. The engraving is an unusual record of the process.

The most puzzling part of the inscription is also the most fascinating: 'Hawarth me wrought and Brand priest.' A literal interpretation of this is: 'Hawarth made me [the sundial], and Brand is the priest.' Thus we know who made the sundial almost 1,000 years ago, and who was the priest at the time. Brand's identification on the stone makes him the first parish priest known by name in Yorkshire. Some people claim that the inscription refers to more than one priest, for the word is abbreviated as 'prs'. But this seems equally acceptable for one priest as for more than one, and the sense of the inscription suggests there was only Brand.

The sundial was discovered in its present position under a layer of plaster in 1771, but no one can be sure it has always been there. Most Saxon churches did not have a south door, and the original entrance to St Gregory's was almost certainly by the church's fine western arch, now inside the church and leading to a bell tower built in 1827. There is also evidence that the wall containing the sundial was rebuilt more or less completely in Norman times, when the south doorway was inserted. That the Normans chose to have the sundial above their new doorway is obvious. But whether the stone was already conveniently positioned for the job or had to be moved from elsewhere will probably never be known. The matter is complicated by suggestions that the dial might originally have been in the chancel wall, in which case it would probably not

142

have been moved until a major rebuilding of the chancel in the thirteenth century. In 1959 the Kensington Science Museum made a cast of the sundial, and replicas now exist in several other museums in Britain and abroad.

Although St Gregory's was extensively rebuilt in Victorian times, with a further restoration in 1907–9, visitors can see many links with Orm's church of about 1060. Apart from the sundial and the original entrance, the whole of the lower part of the western wall appears to be the work of Orm's masons. The evidence is some characteristic Saxon long-and-short work— the placing of certain stones with the long sides alternately horizontal and vertical. This ends abruptly at part of an eleventh-century Danish cross, built into the exterior of the wall about 9ft from the ground.

Inside, the shafts to the chancel arch are Saxon. Especially worth noting are the stone wall benches, the earliest form of church seating: benches such as these are the origin of the phrase 'the weakest go to the wall'.

Among several Saxon stones kept loose in the church are two handsome graveslabs, one carved with a cross and the other showing a delicate interlace pattern. Both are pondered over almost as much as the sundial. Until the restoration of 1907–9 they were embedded in the west wall, and when they were removed some parishioners claimed that the stone with the cross used to have a weathered inscription in memory of King Ethelwald. If true, this supports an old theory that Kirkdale was the site of a monastery founded by St Cedd, a Northumbrian missionary priest, for Ethelwald is known to have asked Cedd to build a monastery in which his body might be buried.

Enthusiasm for this theory led to a claim that the second stone was the gravestone of Cedd himself. Most experts now say that Cedd's monastery was at Lastingham, but speculation about the stones continues. A recent suggestion is that when Lastingham fell to Danish raiders in the ninth century, the sacred remains of Cedd and Ethelwald could have been moved to Kirkdale, where new gravestones were made. Whatever the merits of this theory, the early missionary settlement

143

at Kirkdale most probably suffered the same eventual fate as Lastingham, thus ending its days as a 'minster'.

The church's isolated position, with not even a farmhouse in sight, has prompted some curious stories. One tale is that the church was to have been built at either Nawton or Wombleton, but the stones delivered for the job twice disappeared and turned up at Kirkdale. A variation is that the builders worked at the intended site but during the night the completed portions moved to Kirkdale and assembled themselves into a church.

In St Gregory's churchyard are two gravestones that I admire. One, in memory of W. R. Wood, who died in 1953, says: 'Cricket he loved; cricket he lived.' A stone dating from 1974, to Major R. H. D. Fabling, is engraved: 'Your Marker. A symbolic tribute.' This is a subtle reference to the final line of the sundial's inscription, which says: 'This is day's sunmarker at all times.'

People who make a return visit to St Gregory's sometimes receive a surprise. They may find that Hodge Beck, previously observed to be rushing along in a gorge on one side of the churchyard, has disappeared, or that what was formerly a dry channel has become a sizeable stream. These changes occur because near Hold Cauldron, a mile or so upstream from St Gregory's, the Hodge becomes subterranean, rising above ground only after heavy rainfall.

A very attractive walk leads from the church past Hold Cauldron Mill to Sleightholmedale, where the valley of the Hodge opens into a sylvan landscape of woods and meadows, centred on a lovely country house, Sleightholmedale Lodge. Further north the valley changes its character—and its name—yet again. It becomes Bransdale, a sturdy farming dale, much of which was acquired by the National Trust in 1972. An oddity of the Trust's careful management are some traffic notices, requesting motorists to park *on* the grass verges—the opposite of the usual instruction. The explanation is that there is an abundance of verge and very little road.

St Gregory's sundial was probably the inspiration for a surprising number of sundials scattered throughout Bransdale.

Some, attached to farms, are thought to have been the work of a Victorian named Mr Moon. A freestanding dial is concealed behind the roadside wall near the ruined chapel opposite Cornfield House. A more impressive counterpart stands incongruously in a field west of Bransdale Mill. Dated 1819, this is engraved with the name of William Strickland, whose family once owned the mill. Other sides of the pillar record the names of the masons, John Brown and Joseph Wood, and there is a motto in Latin and English: *Quota Hora Est Vide*—Time and Life Move Swiftly. The nearby mill, in use until 1935, is said to have been the only oatmeal mill in the North York Moors. William Strickland's initials appear in large iron letters on the side.

Among the people fond of all this countryside, and especially St Gregory's Minster, was Sir Herbert Read, the poet and art critic. As a child he travelled to the church in a dogcart from his home at Muscoates Grange. He later lived at Stonegrave, near Helmsley, and when he died in 1968, the funeral service was held at St Gregory's.

In October 1970 Sir John Betjeman attended Evensong at St Gregory's and read some of his poems from the pulpit. I am sure Sir John would approve of a poem about the church and its surroundings by Ronald Scriven, Yorkshire's very fine poet, who is both blind and deaf. For me it perfectly evokes the atmosphere of this timeless place:

> Over the porch
> of Kirkdale church
> the old Norse sundial
> has to search
> for gleams of the sun
> which used to scorch
> its stone in summer.
> The weathered face
> is long resigned
> to Time's slow pace.
> Time in winter,
> the rogue, the knave,
> falls asleep in Kirkdale Cave.
> I hope his dreams

are haunted there
by ghosts of mammoth
and cave bear,
to pay him out,
the capering mummer,
for his galloping speed
in spring and summer.

St Mary's, Whitby

Sir Nikolaus Pevsner, the architectural writer, calls Whitby's parish church of St Mary 'one of the churches one is fondest of in all England . . . hard to believe, impossible not to love.' A few years ago, much the same thought was put in a slightly different way by Whitby's rector, Canon Joe Penniston, who said: 'While a few people might be willing to blow up St Mary's, to many others it is the most remarkable place on earth.'

Poised on the cliff edge high above the harbour, the church almost sails over the old town. From the streets of Whitby it is St Mary's rather than the abbey that most often forms the focus of the many beautiful views. From parts of the clifftop, notably near the abbey itself, the church appears incredibly huddled and compact, like a ship bracing itself against a storm.

The nautical resemblance is more than accidental. St Mary's once had a pitched roof, the outline of which can be seen on the eastern wall of the tower. When a new roof was needed in the seventeenth century, ships' carpenters were called in. They made St Mary's waterproof in the way they knew best, by providing a roof not unlike the deck of a ship. During later alterations, in about 1819, long rows of ship's cabin skylights were inserted into this roof. The result is that to stand in the nave of Whitby's parish church is about as close as you can come on dry land to being below decks on an old sailing ship. Can any town show a deeper bond with the sea?

The intimacy of St Mary's makes it hard to realise that the church can seat 2,000 people—as many as an Odeon cinema of the 1930s. The secret lies in what Pevsner calls 'the unmatched crowding and confusion of the interior', crammed with galleries and box pews. Some pews are set aside for church officials while others are marked with the names of prominent families or nearby parishes, reflecting St Mary's role as the 'mother' church of the entire Whitby district. One or two pews bear the forbidding words 'For Strangers Only'.

Erected earlier than any of these is a pew as sumptuous as a box at the theatre. Raised on barley-sugar columns, it straddles the centre aisle—the bridge of this particular ship. It was erected in about 1620 for the squire, Sir Hugh Cholmley, and although it masks a fine Norman chancel-arch its removal is now unthinkable. With its own special entrance from outside—a flight of stairs protected by a wooden canopy—the pew is still used by the current lord or lady of the manor.

A close rival of the Cholmley pew is a three-deck pulpit dating from 1778. The bottom deck was occupied by the parish clerk, the middle deck by the minister, and the top deck by the visiting preacher. Attached to the lofty structure are ear trumpets, placed there by the vicar of 1809–43 to ensure that his deaf wife, in the pew below, did not miss a single word of his sermons.

Behind the pulpit is one of England's few surviving jade pews, the ecclesiastic version of the stocks. The pew was set aside for women who had committed certain offences, notably adultery. Dressed in a shroud and carrying a wand, the hapless jade was made to walk barefoot to the pew and listen to an address calling on her to repent.

In many other ways St Mary's asserts its individuality. Extensions long ago caused the church to lose the traditional cruciform shape. The many Georgian windows, inserted between about 1740 and 1764, make no concession to church style but are simply good domestic windows of the period. St Mary's is also believed to be the only parish church in England without an altar: at its heart is a magnificent oak communion table, dating from at least the time of Queen Elizabeth I.

Stranger still, a model of a Greek temple stands in the porch, the official memorial to the dead of the 1861 Lifeboat Disaster (see p 85). Since Greek temples are dedicated to pagan gods, models of them are not usually found in Christian churches. The history of St Mary's model is that the minister in 1861 saw it in a shop in Marylebone, and selected it as the lifeboatmen's memorial.

St Mary's was crowded for the lifeboat-disaster memorial service, conducted by the Rev William Scoresby, Whitby's whaling-skipper-turned priest (see p 45). The bishop's chair, which is dedicated to him, is made of timber salvaged from the wreck of a ship in which he had earlier sailed to Australia to test a compass he had invented. The carvings on the chair include the Scoresby arms and the scene of the shipwreck.

With the church still lacking electricity, regular services are confined to the lighter months. For special evening services at other times, such as at Christmas, the church is lit by 240 candles, which fill the church with beauty and create what most worshippers agree is a deeply moving atmosphere.

Although there is a road to St Mary's, most visitors arrive by climbing Whitby's famous 199 steps, known as Church Stairs. They belong to St Mary's and not to the abbey as is commonly believed, and are perhaps the most amazing approach to any parish church in England. No one is sure when steps to the church were first cut, but a wooden stairway is known to have existed in 1370. At an unknown date this stairway was strengthened by stone supports. The stone steps themselves may have been installed between 1750 and 1770 when 103 tons of stones were delivered to the church since no other project is recorded for that period to account for the use of the stone.

The number of steps has varied over the years. In 1777 and 1817 when Lionel Charlton and George Young respectively published their histories of Whitby, the total was 190. Young, however, states that the original 195 steps were reduced by repairs. Today's intriguing total has remained constant since at least late Victorian days when a race up and down the '199 steps' was a yearly summertime attraction. In 1977 the race was revived by BBC Radio Cleveland which announced that it might again become an annual event. Potash worker David Pybus, of Whitby, panted home in 32 seconds.

People in no hurry to reach the top often sit on the benches beside the steps. Few realise that these are not seats but coffin rests. Although no longer used for this purpose, they were provided to allow bearers to recover their breath—and their strength—on the steep climb to the churchyard. I have also been told that a lamp-post on the steps today serves as a navigational aid to vessels entering the port.

Near the top of the steps is a cross to Caedmon, England's first hymn-writer or, as it is sometimes put, 'the father of English sacred song'. According to Bede, Caedmon, a shepherd boy, dreamt that a stranger said to him: 'Caedmon, sing some song to me.' After protesting that he could not sing, Caedmon asked: 'Of what shall I sing?' On being told to: 'Sing of the beginning of Creation' Caedmon sang a beautiful hymn, which he repeated the next day to monks at the abbey. His cross, set up at the instigation of Canon Rawnsley, a founder of the National Trust, was unveiled in 1898 by the Poet Laureate, Alfred Austin.

Along the cliff path from the Caedmon Cross are the graves of some of the 1861 lifeboatmen. Landslip was once common in this part of the churchyard, and there are tales of coffins appearing as the earth fell away.

This ghoulish phenomenon well suits the churchyard as a setting for scenes in Bram Stoker's novel *Dracula*. Stoker (1847–1912) wrote part of his great horror story while staying in a house in Whitby's East Crescent in about 1896. In the novel, Dracula survives a shipwreck and comes ashore at Whitby's Tate Hill pier in the form of a large dog. He races up the 199 steps, slakes his thirst on a young girl visitor and takes refuge in a suicide's grave. These events were re-enacted on the spot in 1930 during the making of *Dracula*, perhaps the best film version of the celebrated tale, with Bela Lugozi as the Count. During breaks in filming, Lugozi sometimes sat on a bench overlooking the harbour, smoking a cigarette. There are reports of unsuspecting holiday makers being startled by the cloaked and fanged figure. Stoker's novel, incidentally, includes some underrated descriptive passages about the town.

Almost in keeping with the Dracula legend are two large sandstone slabs alongside the pathway between St Mary's and the abbey. Engraved only with a skull and crossbones they mark the graves of pirates. Nearby, in the pathway on the south side of the church, is a small tablet to P. S. Hubbersty. This nine year old girl was killed in 1810 when she fell from the cliffs while playing with her sister. Many years later, the sister, dying in old age, confessed that she had pushed the girl over in a tantrum.

The most memorable of St Mary's many memorials is a gravestone in a niche in the outside church wall. It tells of Francis Huntrodds and his wife Mary, who were both born on the same day 19 September 1600. Married on their birthday, they brought up 12 children and died, aged 80, also on their birthday within 5 hours of each other. Their epitaph is one that I and many other admirers of St Mary's never tire of reading:

> So fit a match surely could never be
> Both in their lives and in their deaths agree.

Lastingham

In about AD700 the venerable Bede described Lastingham as being 'among lofty and remote mountains in which there appeared to have been more of the lurking places of robbers and dens of wild beasts than habitations of men'. Nevertheless, it was to this inhospitable spot that St Cedd, schooled as a missionary at Lindisfarne, had arrived only four or five decades earlier to set up a monastery. Although Lastingham Church does not date from the start of that community, its history is closely tied to it—in fact, it is one of the few parish churches in England that might also be said to be an abbey!

Cedd's monastery, built in 655, was a simple wooden building surrounded by an earth rampart. When Cedd died in 664 his body was buried within the precincts of the monastery. Shortly afterwards, a stone church was built and Cedd's remains were reinterred by the altar.

150

Within the next 100 years the monastery was probably destroyed by invading Danes. At any rate, no record of it exists from the eighth century until 1078, when Abbot Stephen of Whitby, whose own abbey was under threat, decided to move to Cedd's former retreat at Lastingham.

The physical story of the present church begins there—and it is a remarkable one. Stephen's first task was to build a crypt in which to place the sacred remains of Cedd. This crypt, a miniature church complete with chancel, nave, and two side aisles, splendidly survives beneath today's church. Permanently open to visitors, it is one of Britain's finest examples of late eleventh-century architecture.

The most impressive features of the crypt are its immensely strong Norman columns and vaulted roof. The only changes in the last 900 years have been the levelling of the floor, the application of plaster between the ribs of the roof, probably to replace decayed wooden panelling, and the insertion of stairs to provide access from the church. The crypt's original doorway, now blocked up, was in the north-west wall. This allowed pilgrims to visit the Cedd shrine without interrupting worship in the church.

The crypt was intended to be the beginning of an abbey, for which Stephen next built a semi-circular apse. Now forming the east end of the church, this echoes a similar but smaller apse in the crypt. The chancel and the large pillars in the nave were also put up as part of the abbey. It seems likely that the whole area of the present building was planned to be merely one part, probably the chancel, of a much larger building. The main body of the abbey would have been added beyond today's west wall.

But Abbot Stephen badly misjudged Lastingham as a place of refuge. It obviously still held some of the terrors of Bede's day, for the monks were so severely harassed by marauders that after only ten years they moved to York, where they founded St Mary's Abbey.

For the next 142 years only minimal duties were performed at Lastingham, by a priest sent from York. But the appointment of a vicar in 1230 indicates that a decision had been taken to turn Stephen's partly completed abbey into a parish church. The conversion brought an interesting marriage of styles, for the spaces between the Norman columns were filled with pointed English arches rather than the round arches of true Norman buildings. Extra pillars were needed and these are easily identified since they are more slender than those of the Norman period.

It was at this time, too, that the west wall was built. It incorporates a pair of the Norman columns, which protrude beyond the outer face of the wall, marking the place where the abbey's transept, or main crossing, would have been. Had it been built, the abbey's central tower would have risen above this spot. The side aisles were also added to the building during its conversion to a church, but after about 100 years the south aisle was widened, in a programme that included the construction of the present tower.

In 1831 the church received astonishing treatment at the hands of John Jackson, the son of a Lastingham tailor. Becoming distinguished as an oil painter, ultimately elected to the Royal Academy, Jackson painted a copy of Correggio's 'Mount of Olives' and presented it to his village church. To create enough space for the painting in the apse, he had the Norman windows filled in. He then inserted a skylight of yellow glass and, most incredibly of all, he replaced the altar with a circular card table. Fortunately, these garish changes, calculated to make the church resemble a Greek temple, were remedied in a general restoration of 1879 by John L. Pearson, the architect of Truro Cathedral. Particularly notable is Pearson's roof, in the style of the crypt. The work was commissioned by Dr Ringer, the local family doctor, in memory of his young daughter, Anne.

Another unusual episode occurred in the eighteenth century when the wife of a curate kept the village pub, the Blacksmith's Arms. The curate, Jeremiah Carter, played his fiddle in the pub on Sundays. When the archdeacon demanded an explanation, Carter sent this stout reply:

. . . as my parish is so wide that some of my parishioners have to come from ten to 15 miles to church, you will readily allow that some refreshment before they return must occasionally be necessary, and when can they have it more properly than when the journey is half performed? Now, sir, I make no doubt but you are well assured that the most general topics of conversation at public houses are politics and religion, with which ninety-nine out of a hundred of those who participate in the general clamour are unacquainted; and that perpetually ringing in the ears of the pastor who has the welfare and happiness of his flock at heart must be a sore mortification.

To divert their attention from these foibles over their cups, I take down my violin and play them a few tunes, which gives me an opportunity of seeing that they get no more liquor than is necessary for refreshment; and if the younger people propose a dance, I seldom answer in the negative: nevertheless, when I announce time for return, they are ever ready to obey my commands, and generally with the donation of a sixpence they shake hands with my children and bid God bless them. Thus my parishioners enjoy a triple advantage, being instructed, fed and amused at the same time.

Carter concluded that his parishioners found this form of Sunday observance 'congenial with their inclinations'. Perhaps the archdeacon agreed, for he took no further action. Jeremiah had an annual stipend of £20 on which to support himself, his wife and thirteen children.

Some people say that the stone altar slab in the crypt could be part of the high altar of the original Saxon church. Also in the crypt is a very large Anglo-Saxon cross-head, and the estimated height of the cross—24ft—makes it the largest known pre-Norman monument in England. Cedd himself might have commissioned it.

The original Ainhowe Cross, whose nineteenth-century replacement stands in Rosedale, is also in the church, and other notable fragments include two short rectangular stones that might have been part of the door frame of the Saxon church. Especially worth noting is the gravestone lintel over the south doorway—perhaps another Saxon relic. The most unexpected item, however, is a small square stone with a hollow in the middle. This is a Roman incense stone which, like others of its kind, had a macabre purpose. Roman soldiers were asked to sprinkle incense on the flame while charcoal burned in the stone, and any soldier refusing to do so was identified as a Christian and executed. The stone was probably used at Cawthorne Camps (see p 79).

The history of Lastingham church spills over into the village. Near the main bridge is a holy well dedicated to St Cedd. The stone for its canopy is said to have been taken from Rosedale Abbey in the nineteenth century. A second well, dedicated to Cedd's brother St Chadd, who became abbot of Lastingham on Cedd's death, stands on the east side of the High Street. A window in the north aisle of the church shows both Cedd and Chadd, the latter standing above a model of the cathedral at Lichfield, where he was appointed bishop. A bridge at the lower end of the village displays an inscription to John Jackson, whose copy of the Correggio painting is still in the church, although not in the apse. Other paintings by Jackson can be seen at Castle Howard and they are a finer tribute to his talents than his preposterous efforts for his parish church.

Pickering

Of the six or seven market towns that form such attractive gateways to the North York Moors, easily the most moorland in quality is Pickering. Much of its character stems from the way its two principal streets rise steeply to the town centre, where the parish church stands. But although its shapely spire is prominent from both the town and the surrounding countryside, the building does its best to remain out of reach. Visitors find that the final few yards of the approach are via narrow gaps in the street, and steps.

The great interest is inside, for the church contains one of Britain's most complete sets of medieval wall paintings. Occupying the whole of the north and south walls of the nave, they were probably painted by a band of itinerant painters in the late fifteenth century. At that time, few people could read, and the paintings were intended to offer pictorial instruction in Christianity—the visual aids of their day. They also helped to create a devotional atmosphere, as stained-glass windows still do today.

The paintings were discovered in 1851 by workmen removing a gallery, but the vicar and the Archbishop of York disagreed about them: the archbishop thought the paintings should be preserved, but the vicar claimed they would distract the congregation and wanted them obliterated. Although supported by most of the population of Pickering, the archbishop lost his fight and the paintings were covered by a yellow wash.

During further work on the church in 1878 the paintings were again brought to light. With a new vicar, the Rev G. H. Lightfoot, wholeheartedly in favour of the paintings, there was no serious dispute that they should stay on view. Unfortunately, the removal of the old yellow wash caused some damage to the paintings, and it is debatable whether the authorities took the proper course in repainting the affected parts. In my opinion, it is preferable for visitors to be able to appreciate the content and purpose of the paintings than to have little to marvel at except sketchy medieval brushwork. Since the paintings are not notable as art, some judicious touching up, to keep the artist's message clear, seems amply justified.

On the north wall, the sequence of paintings begins with St George and the dragon. Then comes a painting of St Christopher, patron saint of travellers, appropriately facing the main door. A former follower of Satan, Christopher repented and carried pilgrims across a river near a monastery. One night, as he carried a child his burden seemed unaccountably heavy. The child observed that Christopher, until then known as Offero, was carrying 'Him who bears the sins of the world.' Offero thus became Christopher, the Christ-bearer. The picture shows him holding the infant while trampling the devil, in the form of a serpent. His use of a tree as a staff, also shown in the picture, is explained by a legend that he was 'twelve cubits high'. Worth noting in the corner of the picture is the lantern-

155

carrying figure of the abbot, guiding Christopher across the stream.

Two series of smaller pictures follow, one above the other. At the bottom are scenes from the story of St John the Baptist. These show John being beheaded, his head being offered to Herod, and finally (out of sequence) John reproving Salome as she performs a sensuous tumble dance.

Above this trio of paintings appears the first of a number of pictures devoted to St Mary. It shows Mary being crowned Queen of Heaven, in the company of God and Christ, who is represented by a dove. At the top of the picture, in what is sometimes mistaken for a separate painting, appears the 'host of heaven'—an angelic choir watching Mary's coronation from the rampart of heaven.

Closer to the altar is a very large painting showing two archers, with a figure lashed to a tree and impaled by arrows. This depicts the martyrdom of St Edmund, the East Anglian king who was captured by Danes in the ninth century. Refusing to renounce Christianity, Edmund met the threat of death by saying, 'I cannot die'—a reference to the life after death. After his murder, his body was buried in a chapel where the cathedral of Bury St Edmunds now stands.

Higher on the wall is a painting of the murder of Thomas Becket. The four knights who committed the crime are seen approaching Thomas, and it is interesting that their coats of arms belong to the years 1450–60. This is important evidence for dating the paintings in the latter half of the fifteenth century.

As the visitor retraces his steps to the church door, the first ten pictures on the south wall are all from the life of St Catherine of Alexandria. A queen at fourteen, she later became a Christian, and when the Romans invaded her country she pleaded with the emperor not to persecute her Christian subjects. Her life is depicted as follows: 1 Catherine meets the emperor; 2 she is sent to prison; 3 she debates Christianity with the emperor's counsellors; 4 furious that Catherine has converted the counsellors, the emperor orders the converts to be killed; 5 Catherine is taken back to prison; 6 stripped to the waist she is beaten in the presence of the emperor; 7 she returns to her cell; 8 she is joined in prayer by the emperor's wife, now also a Christian; 9 the emperor arranges for Catherine to be tortured on a spiked wheel (the origin of the Catherine Wheel), but two angels destroy the wheel and overthrow the guards; 10 Catherine kneels to be executed. This story was the subject of the earliest known miracle play in 1111.

These paintings are followed by a sequence of seven small paintings showing the Acts of Mercy: feeding the hungry, giving drink to the thirsty, sheltering the stranger, clothing the naked, caring for the sick, visiting those in prison, and burying the dead.

A further seven paintings illustrate scenes from the life of Christ. The first four show him healing the ear of Malchus, appearing before Pilate, being scourged, and carrying his cross. The other three pictures show the crucifixion and Christ's body being removed from the cross and placed in the tomb.

In a further picture, squeezed into the space between two arches, Jesus is seen in Hades where, according to St Peter, he preached to people awaiting judgement. Adam and Eve are seen emerging from the mouth of a dragon, representing Death. Clearly intended to be a companion to this picture is an illustration of Christ's resurrection with soldiers fainting as Jesus, flanked by angels, emerges from the tomb.

Rounding off the entire series of paintings are three more devoted to St Mary. The most westerly include six of the disciples and may have been intended to portray the death of Mary. The middle painting certainly depicts her funeral, illustrating the disrespectful act of the Jewish Prince Belzeray who leapt astride the coffin and was unable to climb off until the disciples prayed for his release. The easternmost painting, near the upper windows of the south wall, is incomplete but probably showed Mary being received into heaven. The painters then depicted her heavenly coronation on the other side of the aisle.

The paintings have been restored three times this century— in 1918, 1947 and 1968. The last restoration cost £1,000 and was said to have safeguarded the paintings for the rest of the century.

Pickering church is also notable for its connections with the USA. A tablet in the sanctuary commemorates two Pickering men, Robert King and his son Nicholas, who were leading surveyors in the planning of the USA capital of Washington. From this link have sprung other ties: donations from USA citizens paid for the panelling in the chancel and the choir, and the arms of the USA appear with those of Archbishop Temple of York on the priest's stall.

Another tablet, with an attractive motif of farm implements and a horn of plenty, recalls William Marshall, a key figure in the history of agriculture. Born in 1745 at Sinnington, Marshall was one of the first people to understand the need to organise farming as an industry instead of relying on the haphazard results from thousands of farms, each worked without reference to what was going on elsewhere. Oddly, Marshall farmed for fourteen years in the West Indies before managing a farm at Croydon, Surrey. After touring the country and noting the agricultural practices, including the tools and machines used, he produced a classic series of books, *The Rural Economy of England*. The first of two volumes dealing with Yorkshire was published in Pickering on 21 December 1787.

Marshall's proposal for a Board of Agriculture, forerunner of today's ministry, was carried out by Parliament in 1793. When he died in 1818 he was busy converting his home at Beck Isle, Pickering, into a farmers' school or pioneer 'college of agriculture'. Although now forgotten virtually everywhere except in his native corner of Yorkshire, Marshall was a true man of vision.

9

... AND A CHURCHMAN

Few parts of Britain have produced a richer collection of clergy-men than the North York Moors. Three of them—Jeremiah Carter of Lastingham, John Christopher Atkinson of Danby, and Laurence Sterne of Coxwold—find places elsewhere in this book (see pp 152, 113, and 174 respectively). But even discount-ing the Rev William Kingsley, whose practical joking at Kil-vington, near Thirsk, puts him just beyond the boundaries of the present book, the moorland area can boast at least three more priests who are remarkable by any standard.

Canon Kyle

When Canon John Latimer Kyle died in 1943 he had been vicar at Carlton, near Stokesley, for forty-nine years. He ran three farms, rode with the local hunt, and gained a wide reputation for his down-to-earth humour and the good sense of his ser-mons. Most memorably, he outdid Lastingham's fiddle-playing curate by buying and managing a local pub.

The Fox and Hounds was next door to the canon's vicarage, but Canon Kyle's motive in taking over the pub was not to cur-tail its activities. On the contrary, his enthusiasm for the pub was so great that in 1909 he encouraged his wife to paint the inn sign, one side of which showed a fox going to ground with the hounds in pursuit.

The purchase of the pub brought the canon front-page publicity and some stern opposition. He retaliated by publishing a pamphlet entitled *Why I Keep a Public House*, in which he wrote:

> Say what the reformers will, men always have and always will visit their village pubs to meet each other, to discuss local topics and enjoy games of dominoes and darts. Our country inns play a useful part in the social life of every village. Surely they are better in the hands of those who don't wish to run them solely for profit.

The nearest the canon came to conceding anything to his critics was to refuse to open his pub on Sundays. This resulted in a permanent six-day licence for the Fox and Hounds. But some of the canon's ideas about pubs have only recently gained wide acceptance. His pamphlet explains that the man in charge of the Fox and Hounds was instructed to observe his wish that 'a lad or man who buys only a bottle of pop is as welcome as anyone else, and callers requiring tea or a meal are equally welcome.' Above the stables and coach house of the inn the canon opened one of the country's first youth clubs, doubly remarkable for being in a rural area.

When the canon arrived in Carlton in 1894 the parish had been without a church or a vicar for thirteen years. The previous church, consecrated in 1879, was mysteriously burned down two years later and the vicar, who had designed and built the church, stood trial for arson. Although he was acquitted—and there is no reason to question his innocence—the events left a legacy of depression in the parish. Moving to Carlton from nearby Hilton-in-Cleveland, Canon Kyle boldly set about restoring morale and raising money for a new church which was built within three years. As the text for his first sermon, delivered in the village school, he took the words: 'Stir up we beseech Thee the wills of Thy Faithful people . . .'

Designed by Temple Moore, a London-based architect who did a good deal of work in North Yorkshire, the church owes its dignity and restraint largely to the canon. He resisted demands for stained glass, explaining that he liked windows to offer glimpses of the trees, the hills and the sky. Although some villagers pressed for a brick building, the canon implemented his desire for a stone church by volunteering to meet any financial loss himself. This proved unnecessary, mainly because farmers provided free cartage of the stone, cut from the western slopes of Cringle Moor. It is astonishing to reflect that the church, which is fourteenth century in style, was completed at a cost of only £2,696.

The canon later commissioned the beautiful lych gate. He also raised £800 for a peal of eight bells, each of which bears an inscription. The Annie Gjers Bell is engraved with the verse:

> When e're the sweet church bell
> Peals over hill and dell
> May Jesus Christ be praised.

The inscription on the Strangers' Bell says: 'Be not forgetful to entertain strangers', while the Village Bell has the message: 'Here will I dwell for I have delight therein'. The Children's Bell quotes Wordsworth's line, 'Heaven lies about us in our infancy', and the Wheat Bell gives thanks for 'Good wheat years 1905–06'. The canon persuaded farmers to donate sacks of wheat to pay for the latter bell.

The canon achieved the building of a new school and, on his own land and at his own expense, he also provided a 'parish room' for reading, recreation and meetings. His work extended beyond Carlton, for he took on full responsibility for the neighbouring parish of Faceby, where he enlarged the church. For a time he was also the minister for Bilsdale, regularly making the 9-mile journey on horseback across the moors and often conducting services when drenched with rain.

The circumstances that brought Canon Kyle to North Yorkshire in the first place are very interesting. Born in Wales of Irish parents, he was ordained after graduating from Cambridge University. While serving as a young priest at Llandaff

161

Cathedral, he one day helped an old man into a railway carriage. In return the man offered him 'a poor little country living', of which he happened to be patron and for which no vicar could be found. Thus John Latimer Kyle moved to Hilton—and that was how they managed things in Victorian England.

The canon's immense popularity as a preacher is perhaps illustrated by an extract from one of his sermons. Emphasising the virtues of honesty and plain dealing, he said:

> It's when a man gets the reputation for not being straight and having to be watched that he loses his most valuable possession—character. I once had a ram in a very good class at a show. The judge could not decide whether to place my tup or another first. Eventually a referee was called to assist, and after more examination and discussion my ram was given the premier award. I know the very sound advice of those who show horses and stock—'If you win, say little; if you lose say nothing;' but I was curious to know why the referee had given preference to my entry. He replied to my query, 'Your tup had mair carackter, and carackter counts for a lot, when you're sorting out either sheep or foaks . . .'

The canon's three farms were Hall Garth in Raisdale, Manor House at Carlton, and Potto Grange near Hutton Rudby. A notable breeder of black-faced sheep he became a familiar figure at markets and shows. Once, when a farmer asked him to pray for rain he said: 'John, I wouldn't willingly hurt your feelings, but what your land wants more than rain is muck.' His love of his land was movingly shown by a wreath at his funeral. In the form of a cross made from corn, berries and autumn leaves, it included a card saying: 'With love from Mrs A. Wynne-Finch and his hedges and ditches.' The canon's coffin was carried on a hand-bier through the village to his grave in Carlton churchyard.

After his death, at the age of eighty-seven, the Fox and Hounds remained in the canon's family. But the high cost of bringing the pub up to modern standards led to its closure in September 1969, after which it was converted into a private

house. During a campaign to keep the pub open it was appropriate that a leading part was played by the licensee of
Carlton's only other pub, the Blackwell Ox, for on the reverse
side of her Fox and Hounds Inn sign, Canon Kyle's wife included the Blackwell Ox, in a picturesque view of the village.
Even after sixty years one good turn deserved another, although
this one sadly proved to be in vain.

Father Postgate

Many people are confident that Father Nicholas Postgate, the
'Martyr of the Moors', will one day be canonised. Few would
deny him the honour. His story begins at the now vanished
Kirkdale House, Egton Bridge, where he was born in 1599. The
son of Roman Catholics, he decided as a young man that he
wished to become a priest, but had to study abroad as Roman
Catholicism was banned in England. From 1621 to 1630 he
trained at a seminary in Douai, northern France, after which he
returned to Yorkshire.

For thirty years Father Postgate was a chaplain, or private
priest, to wealthy families at Saxton near Tadcaster, Burton
Constable in the East Riding, and Kilvington near Thirsk. But
as it became more difficult for families to employ their own
priest he moved to his native moors. There, Father Postgate
made his main home in a thatched cottage at Ugthorpe.
Tramping the moors in a brown cassock with a white canvas
cape he ministered to Roman Catholics in a wide area bounded
broadly by Whitby, Guisborough and Pickering, where some
people say he had a second cottage-home.

Father Postgate celebrated mass in a chapel concealed in the
loft of a house at Egton and this chapel remained hidden for 150
years after his death. It was accidentally discovered, carefully
prepared for a service, when a servant girl cleaning a wall
pushed her hand through plaster concealing the old entrance.
Since then the house, on the east side of the bank between
Egton and Egton Bridge, has been known as the Mass House.
In St Hedda's Roman Catholic Church, Egton Bridge, is a

model of the house showing the secret chapel, which was 15ft long and 10ft wide, but only 5½ft high.

Although the authorities probably turned a blind eye on Father Postgate for much of the time, sudden purges made life hazardous for the itinerant priest. Favourite disguises were a gardener and a pedlar. Several priest's holes in the district, one of which survives in Ugthorpe Old Hall, were almost certainly among his hiding-places. Even the secret chapel had its own trap door, leading to an outbuilding.

The remoteness of the Whitby Moors, plus the Catholic sympathies of three important landowners resulted in the fact that more Roman Catholics lived in the Egton–Ugthorpe area during this period than in any other part of Yorkshire. For a time there was a regular movement of priests between Douai and the ruined Grosmont Priory, in which a tenant farmer maintained a rest house or sanctuary, with an escape route to the Esk. The Roman Catholic church today claims that nowhere else in England can so many families be identified that survived the period of persecution in 'unbroken continuity and faithfulness'. This must owe a good deal to the dedicated work of Father Postgate, who is said to have gained more than 1,000 converts.

But tragedy lay ahead for the conscientious priest. In widespread hysteria following the failure of the so-called Popish Plot—an attempt to overthrow Charles II in 1678—a witch-hunt of Roman Catholics was organised. With a £20 reward available for information leading to the capture of any RC priest, a North Yorkshire exciseman named John Reeves could not resist the temptation. Learning that Father Postgate was to baptise a baby at Ugglebarnby he informed on the priest, and on 7 December 1678, Father Postgate, aged seventy-nine and regarded as a kindly old man, was caught carrying out the baptism at Red Barn Farm, the home of Matthew Lyth. The farmhouse is still there, although altered, and Matthew Lyth's family is among those that can be traced to the present day: a direct descendant of Lyth is a schoolteacher in Middlesbrough.

Father Postgate was brought before a magistrate at Brompton, near Scarborough, and then stood trial at York Assizes where, on 16 March 1679, he was sentenced to death. He immediately forgave the two women who had been the only civilians willing to testify against him, and when one of these women later visited him in prison he gave her his last coins to pay for her journey home.

The old man met his death with great dignity. His final words before being hanged, drawn and quartered at York on 7 August 1679, were: 'You know, Mr Sheriff, that I die not for the Plot but for my religion. Be pleased to acquaint His Majesty that I never offended him in any manner . . . I forgive all who have wronged me and brought me to this death, and I desire forgiveness of all people.' A curious twist is that soon after the execution, John Reeves was found drowned, commonly believed by suicide, in a pool on the Murk Esk, near Littlebeck. The pool is now named the Devil's Hole and there is a legend that no fish has been caught there since Reeves' death.

Many personal relics of Father Postgate disappeared soon after his death. But the display in St Hedda's includes part of his prayer-book, a buckle believed to be from his cloak, and his box for carrying the sacraments. Several coins were also recovered from the Mass House, and the secret chapel's collection plate. Rather gruesomely—as some people might think—the martyr's hands were preserved, one now being kept at Ampleforth Abbey and the other at St Cuthbert's Church, Durham. Additional relics in various places include Father Postgate's chalice, which unscrews into three sections, his rosary, and part of the rope with which he was hanged.

All these items were brought together at Ugthorpe in June 1974 for the first of what has become an annual open-air service dedicated to Father Postgate. Organised by the Postgate Society, with the support of Middlesbrough Roman Catholic Diocese, the service is part of a campaign to persuade the Roman Catholic Church to declare the martyr a saint. The church has for many years recognised him as 'The Venerable', an important step towards canonisation.

Roman Catholic congregations around Whitby regularly sing an eight-verse hymn composed by Father Postgate while in prison. A few years ago the Station Hotel, Egton Bridge, was renamed the Postgate in his honour, and at Glaisdale there is a Postgate Farm, which was possibly one of the priest's regular points of call. Many people who have studied the matter are certainly confident that an Ugthorpe farmhouse named the Hermitage occupies the site of Father Postgate's thatched cottage: an ancient wall that is now part of the farm's garage could well be the last surviving fragment of the martyr's home.

Vicar Gray

Few of the people who attend the annual open-air service in the ruins of Rievaulx Abbey could name the man responsible for the event—the Rev Charles Norris Gray, vicar of Helmsley from 1870 until 1913. A powerful, bearded figure, Gray perhaps achieved a greater all-round influence in his parish than any other North Yorkshire priest. Almost from the moment of his arrival he became the district's central figure, eclipsing even Lord Feversham, the major landowner.

There was almost no aspect of local life that Gray left untouched. He introduced one of the country's first parish magazines and used it much less for parish notes than as a means of conducting his own wide-ranging social campaigns. Gray attacked the administration of the workhouse, in particular arguing that workhouse children should wear ordinary clothes rather than a uniform. He pleaded for early closing so that apprentices could play games and enjoy the fresh air. In a long and bitter fight over living conditions, he tackled the combined might of Lord Feversham and the local council.

Gray described some of Lord Feversham's properties as 'utterly unfit for either man or beast'. Frequent deaths from typhoid led Gray to protest at the pollution of the Helmsley's Boro Beck, which served as the High Street's only drain. 'It is plain there is enough filth there to poison anybody,' he wrote.

166

Given wider circulation by a London magazine, his comments prompted improvements that marked the beginning of a sewage system for the town.

Meanwhile Gray concerned himself with the state of Helmsley's roads and footpaths. He highlighted the extra-ordinary situation by which the council allowed stakes for cattle pens to be driven into the footway on market days, the holes afterwards remaining as pitfalls for the unwary. Gray's scathing observations about this, and about streets along which people had to 'slosh, slosh, slosh', were followed by the appear-ance of a steam-roller in Helmsley, heralding work that put the roads and paths into a tolerable condition.

Gray acted as a one-man social agency. He offered advice on how to save coal, on the care of poultry, on workers' compen-sation, and on the feeding of infants. He even cautioned women against the perils of 'tight-lacing', then in fashion. During an influenza epidemic Gray announced that his own favourite antidote, a drink of beef tea and port wine, could be obtained by 'sending up at any time to the vicarage'. He also obtained a better postal service for Helmsley; but another of his cam-paigns—for a public swimming-bath—was not fulfilled until 1970, exactly 100 years after his arrival in Helmsley.

The year in which Gray introduced the Rievaulx Abbey ser-vice is not known. But it might have been connected with an as-tonishing scheme devised by Gray for rebuilding the abbey. Plans were drawn up by Sir Gilbert Scott, architect of the Albert Memorial and that great Victorian building, the St Pancras Railway Hotel. But attempts to raise the £30,000 needed for the Rievaulx scheme were unsuccessful, and the ven-ture was abandoned in 1879.

Gray pressed on with other projects. He opened five churches—at Eastmoors in Bransdale Pockley, Carlton near Helmsley, Sproxton, and Rievaulx. To reach the more outlying of these places for services on Sunday, his curates had to set off on Saturday night. One curate lost his way on Rievaulx Moor and another had to be rescued from a flood at 1.30 am. Gray de-manded so much from his young priests that it was quite common to see them following ploughboys along the furrows.

Perhaps because of his family background—his father was a bishop of Capetown and his grandfather Bishop of Bristol—Gray would tolerate no religious denomination other than his own. On one occasion, when members of his congregation mistakenly donated towards a Methodist project, Gray denounced the affair in his magazine as 'A Clever Dodge'. And when it seemed that Lord Feversham was about to sell land for a Roman Catholic church, Gray wrote to him: 'You are under a distinct promise to me to do nothing in the matter without my consent'—a statement reflecting the exceptional power Gray had assumed. Gray's attitude to the Methodists, incidentally, was in complete contrast to that of Canon Kyle at Carlton near Stokesley. Kyle enlisted Methodist help in paying for the parish church's new peal of bells, and he wrote that the bells would be 'a constant reminder of the help we received from other denominations'.

The annual Rievaulx Abbey service today attracts about 5,000 visitors. It is interesting that Gray drew the same number to Helmsley in 1898 to watch an historical pageant he had organised. The event was a repetition of a similar pageant held the previous year, when more than 3,000 people arrived, mostly on railway excursions from towns throughout the North of England.

In addition to the Rievaulx service, Gray is also remembered for a fine set of wall paintings in Helmsley church. Commissioned by Gray, these depict the history of the parish and the Church of England. Since 1975, the headquarters of the North York Moors National Park has been in the handsome vicarage built by Gray in 1900.

Few Yorkshire people know that Gray was also largely responsible for the restoration of St William's College, a well known half-timbered building near York Minster. Originally the home of chantry priests, the college had degenerated into a row of squalid tenements by the end of the nineteenth century. When a new owner offered to sell the building to the church, Gray leapt in with typical lack of ceremony. Taking action that might perhaps have been expected from the Archbishop of York rather than a country vicar living almost 30 miles away, he sent letters appealing for money to all parts of the country. The result was the preservation of one of Yorkshire's loveliest buildings, which today is used for meetings of the Convocation of York.

10

A HANDFUL OF HOMES

Hamer House

Without the Lyke Wake Walk, the 40-mile trek across the North York Moors, probably few people would have heard of Hamer House. But the slight ruin stands near a popular Lyke Wake Walk staging point on the Egton Bridge–Rosedale road. There the support parties gather; sandwiches and soup are served from the backs of vans and plastic cups defile the moor for half a mile around. Hamer House was once a pub, known as the Lettered Board, and if it never welcomed quite as many callers as the 8,000 or so Lyke Wake walkers who now annually pass nearby, there's little doubt that it attracted a thriving custom.

Hamer flourished as a pub through trade based on the limestone industry, which was established on the southern edge of the moors in the seventeenth century. Lime kilns existed in several places, including Hutton-le-Hole, Cropton, and Beadlam. Farmers from Eskdale journeyed past Hamer to collect lime, taking with them coal dug from pits near their homes. The coal was accepted in part-exchange for the lime and was used to fire the kilns.

The mining of coal in the moors is a little known aspect of the region, but early in the nineteenth century a colliery near Castleton, misleadingly called Danby Pit, employed more than 40 men. Working a 17in seam, which was the broadest in the moors, the colliery produced daily between 200 and 300 bushels (1,600 and 2,400 gal) of coal. Coal was worked in several other places, and Hamer House itself was the centre of a small coalfield. The low spoil heaps are now a series of heather-covered mounds. The last known working of moor coal was on Rudland Rigg and in Rosedale Head during the General Strike of 1926.

Although limestone is still quarried in the Vale of Pickering, lime-burning ceased between about 1870 and 1880. When the barter was at its height, teams of between twenty and forty Galloway ponies, slung with well laden panniers, trailed past Hamer House. Well into this century, elderly dalesmen recalled large herds of these 'gals' grazing on the green at Rosedale Abbey. The leading pony in each train wore a bell, the sound of which helped to keep the other ponies in line. It is also interesting that stone marker posts on many moorland pack-horse tracks were specially scaled down to allow the passage of the pannier-bags. This can be seen on the track above Kirby, near Stokesley, which was also used by coal-carrying teams, serving the local alum industry.

An unusual tragedy once occurred at Hamer House when two travellers died mysteriously during the night without sign of injury or struggle. Since their room had been newly plastered and contained neither fireplace, window, or other means of ventilation they may have been accidentally asphyxiated.

When Hamer ceased to be a pub it continued to be occupied as a house. The last family to live there were the Boddys who left in the 1930s. Among earlier occupants was a large family that made and sold besoms, which they despatched to various markets from Lealholm railway station. The family included twelve children and a dog named Meg. On the command, 'Go fetch them, Meg,' the dog would round up the children. When shown a red handkerchief, always taken from the same drawer, the dog would set off to find the husband, who knew he had to return when he saw the handkerchief tied around the dog's neck.

Life at Hamer, 1,065ft up on the moors with scarcely a bush

in sight, must have been rough to say the least. One man who lived there told how his father once came home with his clothing frozen solid. Lyke Wake walkers passing the spot on a bleak night will need no affirmation of the rigours. Yet Hamer is looked on with affection. So many of its stones have been taken as souvenirs, or perhaps to adorn a suburban rockery, that now little remains except a few low walls, almost submerged in a wave of the turf-topped moor. But even when it has completely disappeared, Hamer will no doubt still steal into the mind's eye, its wildness catching the essence of the moors.

A Roman Villa

A Roman villa sited at Beadlam, just over a mile from Helmsley, is likely to become a popular tourist attraction of the North York Moors within the next few years. Discovered in 1966 and currently being excavated for permanent display, it throws important light on the Roman settlement of the North of England.

The survival of the villa is nothing less than miraculous. Built with the River Riccal as a natural boundary a short distance to the west, it has been further hemmed in over the centuries by the A170 road to the north, the Helmsley–Scarborough railway to the south and a minor road to the east. Despite all this, the site of the villa has remained undisturbed. Easily seen from the main road, the villa seems well placed to take a generous share of the tourist trade enjoyed by the many ancient monuments of North Yorkshire.

The significance of the villa lies in its relation to the pattern of Roman occupation of North-East Yorkshire. Although the Romans had their northern capital at York, and the ruins of an imposing villa exist beneath the turf at Hovingham 7 miles south of Helmsley, the Roman buildings of the moors themselves are all military—Wade's Causeway, the Cawthorne Camps, and two or three coastal signal-stations. As mentioned elsewhere in this book (see p 79), some people claim that the Cawthorne camps were not manned full time—a testimony to their loneliness. Even the Roman town that grew up at Malton was based on the large number of soldiers garrisoned there.

The Beadlam villa gives a fresh perspective to this story. The only villa so far discovered on the northern side of the Vale of Pickering, it provides the first evidence that a settled way of Roman life extended to the very threshold of the moors. Until the discovery of the villa, the existence of an isolated country house in an area remote from principal highways and bordered by a wilderness stretching to the sea would have been seriously doubted. The contradiction of this view indicates that, when the villa was built, there was a high level of security and stability—and prosperity—in the region.

Moreover, the villa is surprisingly sophisticated. In common with only about a quarter of all known Roman villas in England, it boasts a mosaic floor, usually regarded as a token of affluence. This is laid out in a geometric Greek key design, with tiles coloured red, white, blue and brown. The floor has been lifted and stored as a precaution against vandalism, but it will be relaid before the villa is put on view to the public.

Altogether, the villa consists of a three-sided range set around a south-facing courtyard. The domestic portion, which backs on to the moors, is parallel to the A170. The walls stand about 2ft high here and show traces of decorated plaster.

Flanking this block to the east are what will probably prove to be farm buildings, although the area is unexplored at the time of writing. The western wing includes a bath section, in which a number of flue tiles, part of the villa's hypocaust, or underfloor heating system, were found intact and in position. They conveyed warm air to the cavity walls.

The villa was discovered by Mr Tony Pacitto, a well known North Yorkshire archaeologist. Mounds in the meadow suggested the presence of buildings, and when the farmer started ploughing, Mr Pacitto found Roman coins, pottery, and parts of three handmills for grinding corn. A pilot dig soon established the presence of the villa, and two or three further digs took place before work to expose the villa permanently began in 1975. With Mr Pacitto's involvement, the scheme is organised by the Department of the Environment, whose efforts to open the villa to the public at a time when money for such projects is in short supply, deserves great praise.

The villa's occupants probably lived by farming, no doubt finding a ready market for their produce at Malton. The portions of the villa so far uncovered have been dated to the fourth century—the last full century of the Roman occupation. This makes the location of the villa all the more surprising for, by the middle of the century, the east coast had become a serious prey to Saxon raiders, with the Picts also conducting sporadic raids from the north.

Whether the villa was the first house on the site or was raised on the foundations of an earlier building has yet to be decided. But the possibility exists that a peaceable way of Roman life no sooner reached the edge of the North York Moors—a process that had taken 300 years—than it was threatened and then extinguished by barbarian hordes. Particularly exciting was the discovery of a coin dated 390, only twenty years before the Roman armies withdrew from Britain. What happened after that? Did the villa's occupants abandon their comfortable homestead when they heard that the legions had left Malton and York? Or did they remain until the bitter end, gazing out anxiously across Ryedale as the new invaders swept in from the sea?

Shandy Hall

Described by Laurence Sterne as 'my delicious retreat' and 'my philosophical hut', Shandy Hall at Coxwold is claimed to be the oldest, least spoiled home of any great English novelist. It is certainly the only home of any major literary figure within the North York Moors.

Although Sterne has never become quite a household name in Britain, his reputation abroad is as high as that of almost any other English writer. His novel *The Life and Times of Tristram Shandy, Gentleman*, is among the most widely admired books of the world. Sterne wrote much of this comic masterpiece at

Shandy Hall, where he went on to create *A Sentimental Journey*, another book of infectious wit and zest.

The publication of the often bawdy *Tristram Shandy* shocked society—which was shocked anew when it emerged that the author was a country parson. Today, millions of people who have never read a line of Sterne nevertheless laugh with him. As Frank Muir, the humorist and broadcaster, pointed out when he officially opened Shandy Hall to the public, there is scarcely any form of contemporary comedy that cannot be traced back to Sterne and *Tristram Shandy*. In particular, television situation comedy owes a huge debt to Sterne.

Shandy is an old Yorkshire word meaning 'odd' or 'wayward'. Sterne used it to describe his vicarage as well as the hero of his book. The hall is basically a fifteenth-century timber-framed building, a considerable rarity in North Yorkshire. In the seventeenth century it was given an outer case of brick. Sterne arrived in 1760, and from old prints of the hall we know that at that time, as ever since, the building's most distinctive feature has been its huge leaning chimney.

The hall has been appropriately described by Mrs Julia Monkman, wife of the secretary of the Laurence Sterne Trust, as 'a funny cornery sort of house'. Its eccentric character stems largely from its twisting corridors and its twenty rooms, each a different shape and size. Sterne, who rented the house at £12 a year from the Fauconberg Estate, is known to have been responsible for various features that still survive. These include a Georgian niche overlooking a favourite part of the garden, hobgrates with early Adam decoration, and an arched recess that might have been built to contain Sterne's cherished set of blue and white china.

Despite these and other links, by the middle 1960s the house had slipped into serious disrepair. It was then that Kenneth Monkman, a Sterne enthusiast working for the BBC in London, decided that the house must be saved. The Sterne Trust was formed and a world-wide appeal launched. Before the public opening in April 1973, £40,000 worth of work had been carried out.

The result is a Shandy Hall in which Sterne would feel very much at home. Broken windows were replaced with panes of spun glass, of the sort used in Sterne's day: thinner than modern glass, it sparkles more. A stainless steel coil was skilfully inserted into the leaning chimney, strengthening it yet preserving the characteristic profile. The discovery of portions of the original paint on some eighteenth-century panels meant that repainting could be done in similar colours, perhaps those chosen by Sterne.

Gaps in the stone-slate roof—an unusual feature for the moors—were made good with slates from an abandoned farm in West Yorkshire. Decayed areas of brickwork were renewed with hand-made bricks specially produced to match the originals—smaller than the bricks of today. Unfortunately, the doors protecting Sterne's china recess could not be saved, but perfect replicas were made by a York craftsman, Dick Reid. Even Shandy Hall's floors look exactly as they did when Sterne trod them, for worn-out floorboards were replaced with boards of matching oak, cut to the broad width common in Sterne's day.

The first volume of *Tristram Shandy* was published from Coney Street, York, just before Sterne settled at Shandy Hall. When a York bookseller sold 200 copies in the first two days, Sterne was encouraged to write more.

Some of today's readers are puzzled by the anecdotal style of the book, but it should be remembered that Sterne was virtually pioneering the art of novel-writing. A modern literary critic, Katherine Ann Porter, has underlined the special richness of the book by remarking:

> *Tristram Shandy* contains more living, breathing people you can see and hear than any other one novel in the world . . . the fires burning and giving off real smoke, cooking smells coming from the kitchen, real weather outside, and air blowing through the windows . . . and everybody has a navel and his proper distribution of vital organs.

The more earthy aspects of the book are reflected in a comment made a few years after publication: 'How much are divorces multiplied since Sterne appeared.' In the nineteenth century the book earned a famous denunciation from Cardinal Newman, who declared that it had come 'steaming from the hot bed of a lascivious imagination'.

Sterne's great grandfather was an archbishop of York, and although Sterne was born at Clonmel, Ireland, he went to school at Hipperholme, near Halifax. After studying at Cambridge he became a prebendary of York in 1741. Before arriving in Coxwold he spent twenty years as vicar of Sutton-on-Forest with Stillington, near York. It was there that Sterne wrote the earlier parts of *Tristram Shandy*—and it is worth reflecting that the picture of teeming humanity in the book must have been greatly influenced by the author's observations in these two North Yorkshire villages plus, of course, Coxwold: the world in Sterne's personal grain of sand.

Sterne married in 1741, but the marriage did not last and he was alone when he moved to Coxwold. A hint of his character is perhaps contained in an exchange he is said to have had with a Dr John Burton, in Minster Yard, York. During an argument, Burton said: 'Sir, I never give way to a fool.' Sterne replied: 'But I always do,' and waved the doctor on his way. Burton appears as Dr Slop in *Tristram Shandy*.

Shandy Hall is open to the public on Wednesday afternoons in summer and at other times by appointment. The visitor can see Sterne's study, fitted with a library containing his own works and books of the kind he might have used. The room is probably tidier than in Sterne's day, for he is said to have scattered ink wildly in his eagerness to commit ideas to paper. Sometimes, having set off for the village, he would dash back to write down a fresh thought before it escaped him.

Also on view is Sterne's parlour, in which authentic Sterne items include a table, desk, and various ornaments. A section of panelling has been hinged to reveal some early sixteenth-century wall-paintings, discovered during the restoration but probably unknown to Sterne.

The largest room in the house is a huge kitchen, with a

handsome Georgian side oven bearing the Hanover crest. There is also an attractive window seat in a deep recess formed by the chimney. Sterne is thought to have selected his study as the room next to this great chimney, which no doubt generated very welcome warmth.

As a preacher Sterne could fill York Minster. At Coxwold he preached from a three deck pulpit, which has lost a deck since his day. An etching of Sterne, based on a portrait by Sir Joshua Reynolds, hangs in the church vestry, and among other points of interest is a carved boss in the nave depicting a man with an exceptionally long red tongue—a very Shandean image. Not to be missed is the memorable motto of the Bellassis-Fauconberg Families: *Bonne et Belle Assez* (To be Good and Beautiful is Enough).

Sterne disliked what he called the 'thin death-doing pestiferous North-East wind'—a phrase that will appeal to all who live in North-East Yorkshire. But although he suffered greatly from consumption, he died of pleurisy, at the age of fifty-four, while on a visit to his publishers in London. His body was buried in St George's churchyard, Hanover Square, but in 1969, when there was a plan to redevelop the area with flats, his remains were reinterred at Coxwold, where his gravestones can now be seen near the church porch. The later stone, dating from 1793, corrects an error on the first stone about the date of Sterne's death, which was 18 March 1768. The stone also notes 'works unsurpassed in the English language for richness and humour'. The phrase 'Alas Poor Yorick' here refers to the village parson in *Tristram Shandy*.

The removal of Sterne's remains to Coxwold revived an old story that his body was snatched from the grave for anatomical research. Perhaps in confirmation of this the skull recovered from Hanover Square was found to have had its top sawn off. The Sterne Trust believes that the body was snatched but was quickly returned to the grave by Sterne's friends. No one can be sure, however, that the remains at Coxwold are Sterne's. His first gravestone never exactly marked the grave, the inscription merely noting that the body lay 'near this place'. To confuse the

178

issue still further, all the stones in St George's churchyard were moved during World War I to allow the ground to be used as allotments. But the skull recovered from the grave matches the measurements of a bust of Sterne by Nollekens. In any case, Sterne's admirers view the whole affair as he himself would no doubt have wished. As Kenneth Monkman said at the time of the reburial: 'If we've got the wrong remains, no one will be enjoying the joke more than Sterne.'

Yorkshire Thatch

Thatched cottages are perhaps the last feature that many people expect to find in the North York Moors. But thatch provides a pleasant surprise at several places in or near the national park. Pockley, a mile or two from Helmsley, contains the only thatched post office in the county. You need to bend your head to enter the long, low building, and once inside you will look in vain for a postcard of either the post office or the rest of the village, where the charming scattering of thatched homes cannot fail to take the eye: Yorkshire makes little of its natural attractions, and of nothing does it make less than its hidden heritage of thatch.

Before the introduction of pantiles, thatching was the standard means of roofing a house in and around the moors. When George Young wrote his *History of Whitby* early in the nineteenth century he deplored the displacement of thatch by the tiles that today make up the celebrated 'red roofs' of the seaside town. Only one example of coastal thatch now survives—a delightful cottage almost on the sea wall at Runswick Bay.

Inland, the decline of thatch, gathering pace with the Industrial Revolution, is illustrated by an 1868 valuation of Helmsley: while 66 of the town's 256 houses were still thatched, 45 were described as 'old', 'bad', 'very bad', or 'bad old'. By the 1890s only 3 or 4 thatched buildings remained in the town, and Helmsley lost its last piece of thatch when the roof of the old bakehouse in Bondgate collapsed in 1925.

Thatch is still found at Rievaulx, and even in Farndale, a

typical working valley, there are several thatched buildings, including Oak Crag, a medieval house by the eastern road between Low Mill and Church Houses. Among several thatched cottages in Beadlam is one with a garden in which the flowers tumble picturesquely down a bankside towards the road—an especially attractive scene in spring.

One of the most secret of thatched homes is Broadway Foot, by a bridleway between Newgate Bank and Shaken Bridge, near Hawnby. Its thatched chocolate-box dormers are hardly characteristic of the moors, but they make a pretty sight all the same. Spout House (see p 190) by the main Bilsdale road is a more prominent thatched building, and by following a track through Birch Wood, a mile or so to the south, you can also reach the ruin of Carr Cote on the edge of the open moor. Particularly worth noting is its salt box, worn smooth by the hands of many generations.

These and other buildings have attracted increasing attention in recent years not merely because of their thatch but because many are of cruck construction—a style of cottage-building practised from Saxon times until well into the eighteenth century. Several pairs of curved timber struts, or crucks, were erected to form a framework. A large beam was then fixed along the apex of the struts to serve as the roof ridge. Low walls, usually of wattle and daub, were built to the point where the crucks forked sharply inwards. The portion above this became the roof, which sloped to within a few feet of the ground and was generally thatched. This mode of building has been traced to the Schleswig district of Denmark and it was probably introduced to North Yorkshire by Danish raiders of the sixth century.

Pockley Post Office is a cruck house and so are Spout House, Carr Cote, Oak Crag and (although much altered) Broadway Foot. Cliff Cottage, by the A170 at Beadlam, is another example. The cruck-built Star Inn at Harome, a few miles outside the national park, offers a novel opportunity to study the construction method, for coffee is served among the topmost timbers. The subject can also be pursued in the Ryedale Folk

180

Museum, Hutton-le-Hole, where two ruined cruck houses have been rebuilt, one from Harome and the other from Danby Dale.

A cruck house was generally divided in half, the farmer and his family occupying one part with the livestock in the other. The two halves were separated by a passage, with a door at the front and back. On a suitably windy day, threshing by flail took place in the passage, with both doors open to allow the chaff to be blown away. Originally the houses were of a single storey, open to the rafters. With insufficient space to provide separate bedrooms, box-beds were usually inserted into the living area. Later, usually when an upper storey had been squeezed in, most of the box beds were removed. Until at least 1968, however, a box-bed survived as a pantry at Oak Crag. Only the domestic half of this house now stands, with the cross passage incorporated into the living space. The lintel of the passage's former doorway can be seen above a roadside window.

According to folklore, a cruck house for a newly married couple was traditionally built from start to finish on the day of the wedding. In the evening a dance was held in the house to complete the celebrations. Support for these claims came when the two cruck houses were being re-erected at the Ryedale Museum: the volunteer builders surprised themselves by the speed with which they were able to get the heavy timber framework into position.

Cruck houses are by no means peculiar to Yorkshire: in Cumberland they are known as 'clay daubins'. A notable feature of Yorkshire's cruck houses, however, is the inclusion of a 'witch post', intended to ward off evil spirits. Often decorated with carvings of the cross, the post was positioned near the entrance to the main living area and thus had to be passed by anyone coming right into the house. In North Yorkshire it became the custom to cut the post from rowan, a wood associated with protection from evil. The post served the practical purpose of supporting a beam across the ingle-nook.

While the posts are common in Yorkshire, only one has so far been discovered outside the county—at Rawtenstall in Lancashire. On display in the Whitby Museum, Pannet Park, is a jet cross that used to hang on a witch post at Egton. Carved on a post in a house in Glaisdale is a double St Andrew's cross with two sets of initials—probably joint occupiers of the house. A very fine post from Danby, which features a cross embellished with hearts and phases of the moon, is preserved in the Pitt-Rivers Museum at Oxford. Other witch posts stand, or stood, at Lanes Farm, Glaisdale, Bugle Cottage, Egton, and Delves Cottage, Egton Bridge.

At one time, the moorland cruck houses were commonly thatched with heather. Today, the usual moorland thatching material is stalks of wheat, known as long wheat straw. The almost universal use of the combine-harvester, which mangles the wheat stalks, means that supplies have to be gathered carefully from the few farms that still harvest by binder. With the retirement in 1978 of Mr Seth Eccles of Helmsley, Yorkshire's only registered thatcher, the renewal of the county's diminishing stock of thatched roofs, mostly concentrated in the Ryedale area, is likely to become more of a problem. Mr Eccles, who in 1974 spent nine weeks thatching Pockley Post Office, once told me that it takes about five weeks to thatch an average moorland cruck house. Even a good thatch needs to be renewed between every seven and ten years.

Duncombe Park

The stately mansion of Duncombe Park stands at the crest of long meadows that sweep south-westwards from Helmsley Castle. Although most of the building seen today dates from the beginning of this century, its history begins in about 1713, when the first hall on the site was designed by William Wakefield, a squire and an amateur architect, of Huby Hall, near Easingwold. Wakefield followed the style of John Vanbrugh, who had only recently burst on to the architectural scene with Castle Howard—amazingly his first work. For many years it was believed that Duncombe Park was also by Vanbrugh, and some people still say that he advised Wakefield and perhaps even gave him rough plans.

182

In 1845 two wings were added by Sir Charles Barry, architect of the Houses of Parliament. These still stand, together with Barry's gatehouse at Helmsley. However, having been destroyed by two fires in 1879 and 1895, the central block of Duncombe Park was rebuilt to a modified version of Wakefield's original plan by William Young, a local builder. Not surprisingly, he paid special attention to fire precautions, encasing two fire escapes in a pair of battlemented towers that can still be seen.

For all its solid dignity, however, Duncombe Park strikes me as a stern, perhaps even forbidding building. The same cannot be said of its grounds, which are the great glory of this particular 'home'. Embracing the Rievaulx terrace almost two miles away, they have rightly been called 'one of the most extensive and boldest landscaping enterprises in England'.

Their story, like that of the house, opens with Sir Thomas Browne, brother-in-law of Sir Charles Duncombe, a London banker. Sir Charles bought the Helmsley Estate in 1689 after the death of the second Duke of Buckingham. He lived in Helmsley Castle and perhaps also for a time in a house near Sproxton. When he died in 1711, the estate passed to Browne, who changed his name to Duncombe and ordered the building of Duncombe Park.

Browne, one of whose descendants became the first Earl of Feversham, set his mansion where the meadows near Helmsley Castle suddenly give way to steep slopes plunging to the River Rye. To make the most of the splendid position he, or his advisers, decided to create a broad grass promenade along the edge of the escarpment. Still there and beautifully maintained, this promenade curves in a gentle arc for about 600yd in front of the house. It then swings sharply westwards for a further 300yd, tracing a deep meander of the Rye 100ft below.

The significance of this is considerable. Throughout most of the seventeenth century, the gardens of great houses were conceived mainly as polite extensions to the house: they were neat and geometrical, with a well defined boundary not too far from the building. Levens Hall, near Kendal, provides a good example of this kind of garden. But gradually designers came to regard the house as part of the total landscape. At Castle Howard, built mostly between 1699 and 1712, Vanbrugh placed his mansion in a vast parkland; but even so, the avenues and vistas are noticeably formal.

Fifty years later, in the full flood of landscape gardening, men such as Capability Brown created large parklands that are no less contrived but seem part of the natural countryside. Through its use of the contours, and in particular in the way it follows the loop of the Rye, the Duncombe Park terrace reflects an early shift towards this more informal treatment of the landscape.

The point at which the terrace changes direction is marked by a temple, built about 1730 by an unknown architect. An earlier temple, usually accepted as the work of Vanbrugh, punctuates a less obvious change in the terrace at its other end. From here the terrace curls back towards the house as a ha-ha—a level embankment raised behind a specially built stone-retaining wall. Created as a means of gaining height and therefore improving the view, the ha-ha became a popular landscape device throughout England from about 1730. Some people believe, however, that the Duncombe Park ha-ha might well have been completed by, or soon after, 1718 when the house itself was finished. If so, it is one of the first examples of this interesting feature in England.

The elements that distinguish the Duncombe terrace are seen at a higher pitch of perfection in the terrace at Rievaulx. Cut into the hillside above the abbey and completed in 1758, it illustrates the concept of the 'unfolding view'—a series of landscape pictures in a romantic setting. These are obtained through twelve straight avenues, slanted down towards the abbey through a wood. Each avenue offers a different and exquisite perspective on the ruins—a positive agony of choice for any photographer.

Eight hundred unemployed men cut the terrace, the design of which shows great subtlety. With the woodland advancing and receding on both sides, probably few visitors realise that the terrace varies in width from 60 to 100yd. These changes help to sustain interest throughout the half-mile walk along the terrace. It was probably with the same aim in mind that the designer made sure that each end of the terrace is invisible from the other—no mean feat with such a broad promenade, laid out with only the most gentle of curves.

In the 1974 edition of *The Ryedale Historian*, the journal of the Helmsley and District Archaeological Society, Sir Martyn Beckett, a noted architect whose home is in Ryedale, says this about the Rievaulx terrace: 'Nowhere in England have the contours of the land and the views to be seen from them been so originally and successfully used.' Sir Nikolaus Pevsner also says: 'The whole composition is a superlative example of large-scale landscape gardening and of that unquestioning sense of being on top of the world which the rich and fashionable in England possessed throughout the Georgian period.' Pevsner adds that the terrace is unique in focusing on a real ruin rather than the sham structures that other landowners had to erect to obtain similar effects.

In common with the Duncombe Park terrace, the Rievaulx terrace includes two temples. One of them, furnished like a banqueting hall, is open to the public. It is still used occasionally by estate shooting parties, and there is a story, given much local credibility, that the Duke of Kent held his bachelor party there before his marriage to Katherine Worsley, of Hovingham Hall, in 1961. A series of paintings on the ceiling was painted by an Italian while lying on his back. Such paintings were an important feature of classical architecture in England, serving as a substitute for brilliant Mediterranean skies!

In Helmsley it has always been said there was once a plan to link the Duncombe and Rievaulx terraces by a third terrace, which would have been 1¾ miles long and completed an unbroken 'ride' of 3 miles above the Rye. Support for the old story came a few years ago when a quantity of dressed masonry was discovered in a bankside by the Helmsley–Scawton road. This might have been intended for a bridge or viaduct, to take the terrace over a deep gill.

In 1972 the Rievaulx terrace and temples were acquired by The National Trust. Since then The Trust has introduced an excellent walk that takes visitors through the fringe of a wood on the inner edge of the terrace and brings them back along the outer edge, with the views of the abbey in front of them, as they were meant to be seen. The walk passes the original entrance to the terrace from Duncombe Park, still marked by massive gate-posts. At the outer limit of the walk visitors reach the second temple where, by climbing the steps, they can obtain a little known thirteenth view, centred on a stone bridge over the Rye. Wheelchairs are provided for disabled people on this walk, which deserves to be undertaken by every visitor to the North York Moors.

Although the present Earl of Feversham still lives in Helmsley, since 1925 Duncombe Park itself has been leased as a girls' preparatory school. People who ask permission at the Duncombe Park Estate Office in Helmsley, however, are gener-ally allowed to walk freely around the grounds, including the terrace. In common with the free admission to Lord Normanby's grounds at Mulgrave, this is a privilege that deserves respect.

11
TIME OFF

The Old Gooseberry Show

The most precious objects under the sun each summer in the
Esk Valley are gooseberries. In cottage gardens throughout the
dale, protective eyes are turned on the berries that carry their
growers' hopes of winning the top prize at the Egton Bridge Old
Gooseberry Show—one of the most delightful occasions of the
North York Moors.

Nowhere else in the county is there a show devoted solely to
the humble gooseberry, and although a few similar shows are
held elsewhere in the country, mostly in Cheshire, it seems fair
to state that none can match the setting and atmosphere of the
Egton Bridge Show.

Cradled by the Esk in a sheltered part of the valley, with step-
ping-stones and giant Wellingtonias, Egton Bridge is a particularly dream-like place. Gooseberries have been grown and
shown there for more than 150 years, and the result on showday
is berries to make the mind boggle. No gooseberry can hope to
achieve even the mildest glory unless it is at least as big as a
small plum. A golf ball or a bantam's egg is more the size that a
self-respecting berry must attain.

How the Esk Valley gooseberry men encourage the berries
towards this end! Their bushes, which they refer to as trees, are
nourished by ankle-deep manure and protected from birds by
nets or wire mesh. An umbrella, sack or tin is generally also on

hand, to be rushed into use against the extremes of sun, wind and rain. In very dry weather, some growers have been known to fill a boot-polish tin with water and fasten the container beneath a favoured berry, hoping that the evaporation will give the berry a little extra girth and weight. Several growers say they never use a spade, since digging might disturb the roots and impede the bush from putting all its energy into the production of mammoth berries. The most unnerving aspect of the grower's art lies in bringing his berries exactly to their prime on showday. Luck as well as judgement plays a part, for not only hostile weather but a marauding wasp might mean an untimely end for a potential show-stopper.

Always held on the first Tuesday in August, the show is organised by the Egton Bridge Old Gooseberry Society, founded in 1800. All exhibitors must be members, and one of the society's rules is that a new member may not compete with trees formerly owned by another member, except within the same family. Another rule states that if trees are being transferred from one member to another (within the family of course) they must be lifted in the presence of two committee members. The society appoints inspectors who are empowered to carry out spot checks but, happily, cheating is virtually unknown.

Between 1970 and 1977 membership of the society increased from eighty to ninety—treble the total immediately before World War II. Some exhibitors come from well beyond the Esk Valley and (whisper it) even contribute a winning berry or two among the 600 or so on show. The major prize is for the heaviest single berry, but there are also awards for the best berry in various categories, for a pair of berries on a single stem, and for different groupings of berries. Perhaps the most impressive is a group of twelve berries—a union of giants that might tip the scales at over 1lb.

The best known exhibitor of modern times is Mr Tom Ventress. In 1952 he displayed the heaviest berry of the century—a monster weighing almost 2oz. When you meet men like Mr Ventress you quickly learn that a gooseberry is not a gooseberry. It might be white, red, yellow or green. It might be Lord Kitchener, bulbous and bewhiskered, or Lord Derby, with the flushed red cheeks of a clubman. Mr Ventress's world-beater was Transparent, a white berry. In the 1960s Prince Charles appeared, joining an old favourite, Princess Royal. Among other interesting berries, although not now often seen, is Thatcher—yellow, long and smooth, presumably named from its resemblance to a hank of thatch.

The judging ceremony, or weigh-in, is conducted with due solemnity. The weight of the berries is expressed in drams and grains, with the weights themselves being little more than paper-thin flakes of metal. Mr Ventress's immortal berry weighed 30 drams 8 grains. For forty-one years until his death in 1970, Mr Ted Raw of Grosmont, the show secretary, main-tained the society's records in his immaculate copperplate handwriting. He was another great gooseberry man, and it was an honour to be welcomed into his home and see him search out details of old berries as of well loved friends. After his death his daughter Mildred continued exhibiting and in her first season won the class for the heaviest twelve.

Showday is the highlight of the year at Egton Bridge. The berries are carried into St Hedda's Roman Catholic school-room on white plates or in bowls. The prizes are highly prac-tical: tea sets, kitchen ware, garden tools, glasses, towels and blankets. In one recent year there was a clothes' horse. Tea is available for competitors and visitors, and the event is topped off with music by the Stape Silver Band, which travels across the moors from near Pickering.

Afterwards there are gooseberry tales to be told—the won-drous berry that burst on the morning of the show; the man who strained his back lifting his best berry on to a railway wagon. A true story that happened recently concerns a woman from the Esk Valley who was asked if she could send some gooseberry bushes to a former male schoolfriend in Canada. She took the bushes herself, and the reunion of the two friends was soon followed by a wedding. Could there be any better tri-bute to the enchantment of Esk Valley gooseberries?

Spout House

Even though its signboard describes it as the Sun Inn, and the sun's painted rays rise boldly above the front door, the pub in the centre of Bilsdale has always been known as Spout House. To the casual visitor little more than an honest-to-goodness country pub—in itself a rarity these days—it is one of the outstanding places of the North York Moors. Almost every square yard of ground at the modest Spout has its own tale to tell.

The name is derived from a spring that rose on the hillside and emerged near the pub via a stone spout in a boundary wall. Although never used by the present pub, built in 1914, the spout was almost certainly the water supply for the original inn. This low thatched building still stands alongside the 'new' Spout House and is among the oldest buildings in the national park. Excluding the reconstructions in the Ryedale Folk Museum, it is the finest example in the district of the cruck-built long houses once common in the North of England (see p 180). The door opens on to the cross passage that separated the domestic quarters from the section containing the animals, and the interior offers an authentic glimpse of the living arrangement of these important early homes.

Interesting features include space-saving shelves recessed into the wall and an ingle-nook fireplace complete with witch-post, stone-hearth and iron side oven. Nearby is the cottage's original beehive bread oven, damaged but still boasting its stone door. This kind of oven was built into the wall and had neither fire nor flue. Sticks were burned inside, and when the housewife decided that the correct temperature had been reached the ashes were raked out and the dough inserted, to be gently baked by heat radiating from the stone.

Important structural features of the building include its cruck frames and the huge timber saddle that supports the roof ridge. It also has attractive mullioned windows, most of which were put in about a hundred years after the house was built in the sixteenth century. An original mullion survives in the gable facing the road. There is also a handsome window with ten lights, big enough for a small manor house. This suggests a degree of wealth by the occupants who put it in.

If permission is sought from Mr William Ainsley, the Spout House owner and licensee, visitors may be allowed to look inside this historic building, used since the opening of the new pub as an outbuilding of the small farm attached to Spout House. Mr Ainsley's family has been at the Spout since at least 1800, and William Ainsley Senior was born in a box-bed still to be seen at the top of the cruck house's tiny flight of stairs. The last person born in the house was Mr Ainsley's sister Margaret, in 1911. She became Mrs Wilson of Hawk House, Bilsdale, and died in 1970.

The eldest male Ainsley is always christened William and, by tradition, becomes licensee at Spout House. He will probably also take on the secretaryship of Spout House Cricket Club—for the pub has its own eleven in the Helmsley-based Feversham Evening League, even though Bilsdale's only sizeable village, Chop Gate, also runs a cricket team.

The passer-by might wonder where the Spout House men play, for despite the evidence of a stone roller in the meadow behind the pub, no pitch is immediately visible. The explanation is that the Spout House wicket is cut at such a sharp angle into the steeply sloping field that it cannot be detected from the main road at the foot of the bank. The fieldsman standing down the slope at point or square leg stares almost into the blade of the bat. Hen huts occasionally punctuate the outfield, and it needs a relay of two strong men to throw the ball uphill to the stumps from the bottom boundary wall.

But the cricket square is well cared for, and cricket at the Spout surely goes to the roots of the game. In 1974 film cameramen arrived at the pub to record its cricketing activities for a nationally screened BBC television programme. The tradition behind the team is illustrated by a memorial built into the wall on the topside of the field. Engraved with two sets of stumps it is dedicated to Mr Ainsley's grandfather, who died in 1959, aged 84. This remarkable man was cricket secretary for 72 years,

191

which must be a record, especially since he started at 12. His son, the present Mr Ainsley's father, was a fast bowler, and it is said that a clothes' line inside the boundary had to be propped up to accommodate his run.

A memorial to another Spout House cricketer stands by the pub's front door. This memorial is a cross, on the base of which appear the words: 'Also wicket-keeper for Spout House cricket club for many years.' The player was Bobby Dowson, but his chief claim to fame is much less as a cricketer than as a hunting man, for the main part of the inscription states that he was whipper-in to the Bilsdale Hunt for sixty years.

Founded in the seventeenth century, the hunt adds a further vivid strand to the Spout House story. With the neighbouring Sinnington Hunt as one of its rival contenders, the hunt is among claimants to the title of England's Oldest Hunt. Sorting out the facts is far from easy. While there is no evidence that hunting was formalised in Bilsdale before 1680, the year in which a pack of foxhounds is said to have been formed at Sinnington, many people claim that Bilsdale farmers began taking their dogs on foxhunting expeditions before the idea spread to Sinnington. Either way it is likely that both hunts were founded by Helmsley's rakish Duke of Buckingham, and there is no doubt that for many years, perhaps even centuries, the Bilsdale Hunt kennelled its hounds and had its headquarters at Spout House.

The most famous hunting man is Dowson, who is still talked about in Bilsdale although he died in 1902. His funeral at St Hilda's Church, Orra, was an astonishing affair. I have seen old photographs that show how Dowson's horse was led to the churchyard with the dead man's hunting boots fixed upright in the stirrups and his hunting clothes laid across the saddle. I've also been shown a contemporary diary, kept originally by a Bilsdale gamekeeper, describing how Dowson's coffin was followed to the church by 'six redcoats, six greycoats and three couples of hounds'. Dowson's whips, spurs, boots and cap were placed in the grave, and a hunting horn was blown three times. An entry in the diary two years later records the sale of stock

192

and equipment at Dowson's former home, Low Bracken Hill. The huntsman's worldly possessions realised £100—'a good sale,' says the diary.

Dowson's cross at Spout House was intended to mark his grave, but the vicar objected to the motif of a fox's head and hunting whips. For twelve years the cross lay outside the churchyard until followers of the hunt had the idea of putting it by the entrance to the new pub, then being built. Today the cross is a well known curiosity, but scarcely any of the people who stop to look at it bother to search out the much smaller cross, mounted on a rubble base, that identifies Dowson's grave. By kneeling in the grass and scratching the inscription with a nail, you can just decipher this weathered epitaph to the eighty-six year old huntsman:

> No finer sportsman ever followed hounds
> O'er moors and fields he knew for thirty miles around.

Highly prized in North Yorkshire are prints of a painting that portrays the huntsmen of Dowson's day drinking in the old Spout House before setting off for a day on the moors. All the characters are painted from life, with pride of place given to the wiry, irascible-looking Dowson, shown leaning forward to pour hot water from a kettle on the hob into his whisky. Sunlight streams through the large mullioned window where a little girl kneels on the window seat. She later became Mrs Ruth Noble and lived at Hollin Bush Farm, just across the fields from the pub. She was the last member of the group on the painting to survive, dying in the late 1960s.

Painted by a Northumberland artist named Ralph Headley, this picture was once used to advertise Bovril. Some people say that the original painting was held by the family controlling Bovril and was destroyed by a bomb in World War II. There is also a belief that Bovril's use of the picture, in which the trade name was embossed in the bottom right-hand corner, led to a copyright row. At any rate, the Sun Inn's (very faded) copy was kept out of sight for many years, though it now hangs at the bar.

193

The Ainsley family also owns a very fine print without the Bovril name—one of only ten known to exist. Rarer still is a companion painting by Headley dated 1902 and showing the huntsmen outside the inn. The only known copy is in a house in Weardale, County Durham.

This might hardly seem the best moment to disclose that Spout House is not really Spout House—even forgetting that it is also the Sun Inn, but the deed must be done! The official Spout House, recognised as such by the Post Office, among others, is neither the old nor the new pub, but an unassuming cottage immediately to the north. How did this happen? It seems likely that the first building on the site took its name from the nearby water spout. This might well have been the ancient cruck house which, on becoming an inn, transferred its name to the neighbouring cottage. This is doubtful, however, because an old flagged path from the cruck house to the water spout, now grassed over, does not lead there directly but first joins a path alongside the cottage.

Since no one seems to mind that the name remains attached to the pub, it is probably wise to let sleeping dogs lie—except to point out that the long link between the Ainsley's and the Sun Inn is echoed by a similar connection between a family named Weatherill and the official Spout House. Although the cottage has now changed hands, the Weatherills can trace their occupation from 1777 until the 1960s. The late John Weatherill was a master mason at Rievaulx Abbey, and it was largely through his knowledge that historians were able to piece together a history of the abbey masonry—identifying various quarries from which stone for the abbey was cut. John's cousin, Frank, was a mason at Danby where his work includes the Elgee Memorial and the restored Ralph Cross, which he reassembled after it was broken by a man climbing to the top. Another Weatherill, Bill, became an accomplished woodcarver, despite losing an arm in World War I, and an excellent dialect poet.

Bill once told me that his father, who was born at Spout House, used to walk each Christmas into neighbouring dales to collect geese. One of his calls was at the home of Peg

Humphrey, a Bransdale women reputed to be a witch—but Bill's father never saw or heard anything remarkable. A field near Spout House is still named Goose Garth, probably because the geese were gathered there before being driven to the markets of Cleveland and Ryedale. Another field was the scene of one of the first demonstrations of mechanical grass-cutting in the North York Moors. Afterwards, the farmers adjourned to the Sun Inn and declared that the grass would never grow again because it had been brayed to death. This story is just another tiny fragment of history which makes up the rich tapestry of Spout House.

Quoits

Visitors passing through the moorland villages around Whitby on a summer's evening might be surprised to see a cluster of people on a village green; closer investigation will reveal that a quoits' match is in progress. It will be a dull individual indeed whose interest does not quicken when he sees the heavy iron quoit curl through the air, to be followed by the robust clang of metal on metal and the eager cries of the quoiters and their supporters as they gather around the pin.

Few parts of England have kept the game more alive than the Whitby district, where about twelve teams form a thriving quoits league. The settings are always attractive and often beautiful. At Lealholm the game is played on a green with the River Esk alongside and the Board Inn little more than a good quoit's throw away. At Beck Hole, the green with its two quoits pitches is raised like a dais amid exquisitely grouped cottages. Photographs of quoits' teams adorn the walls of the nearby pub, the Birch Hall Inn, and a cottage across the green sports a quoit as a door-knocker. This cottage is still named the Lord Nelson from former days as an inn. It was also for a time the home of Sir Algernon Newton, an accomplished Victorian oil-painter and father of Robert Newton, the actor. A painting by Sir Algernon, depicting the scene upstream of the village bridge, hangs outside the Birch Hall Inn.

There is much more to quoits than meets the eye. What most impresses the casual spectator is the quoit thrown cleanly over the pin or hob—a 'ringer' in quoiting terms. Any advantage gained by this throw is eliminated if a rival player also lands his quoit over the pin. Players therefore employ a wide range of throws to 'fence in' the pin and give their quoit possession.

The quoit itself is not simply a flat iron ring but is saucer-shaped, with the centre punched out. It thus has an inner and an outer slope, referred to as 't'hole' and 't'hill'. One of the best throws, equivalent to a yorker in cricket, is the 'hole gater'—landing the quoit with its inner slope against the top of the pin. Not only does the quoit act as a 'gate', preventing access to the pin, but its round outer slope efficiently deflects oncoming quoits.

Older players say that 'hole gater' throwing is not what it used to be. Quoitsmen are now more likely to use the 'hill gater', also thrown to land in front of the pin but less effective than the hole gater because it presents its inner rather than its outer slope to the next quoit. Its deflective power is thereby reduced.

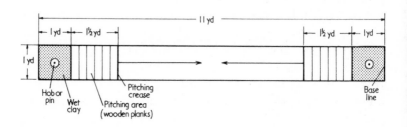

Several other throws may be used, including 'pot' and 'Q', aimed at the sides of the pin, but all throws depend for their effectiveness on a yard-square patch of clay that surrounds the pin. To the quoiter this is holy ground, and it is blasphemy to refer to the clay as 'mud'. During the match, the clay is frequently re-levelled with a special spade. When not in use it is protected by a cover. Some clubs pay a player or a supporter to look after the clay, the condition of which is a source of much comment and concern among quoitsmen. A few years ago Danby experimented with linseed oil on its clay. The verdict was that the clay retained its moisture for longer but the quoits were harder to clean.

Scoring at quoits is the same as in bowls, with twenty-one points for a win. Attributes of the successful quoiter are suppleness of wrist, quickness of eye, judgement of distance—and strength, for although quoits can vary slightly in size and shape, the average quoit weighs $5\frac{1}{4}$lb, and it has to be pitched about $8\frac{1}{2}$yd. In 1971 there was a crisis when several players were unable to replace worn-out quoits. The British Steel Corporation on Teesside came to the rescue, making forty sets—two quoits per set.

A legendary quoits player is the late Arthur Stamford, of Beck Hole. He reputedly pitched sixteen hole gaters in a row—an astonishing feat. William Newton, also of Beck Hole, played into his eighties in the 1960s. A notable quoitsman of more recent years is Terry Smith, one of five brothers who at one time turned out simultaneously for Sleights. In 1971 he set up a record by winning three individual championships in three weeks. Played on Saturday afternoons, usually with a public tea, these championships are among the most enjoyable quoiting occasions. Anyone can enter, and although the tyro will soon be knocked out, he can sample the pleasure and skill of the game.

The most popular theory for the game's origin is that it started with lads throwing horseshoes while waiting at the blacksmith's. Another suggestion is that it evolved from a game brought to England by soldiers after the battle of Agincourt. This would help to explain the term 'Frenchman' for one kind of throw. Yet another theory is that the game is a modified form of discus-throwing.

While individual championships rarely attract fewer than about 50 entries, the number of players in each club has been reduced from 11 to 9. Elderly players recall having to wait long hours for a throw in their youth and of walking 4 or 5 miles to a match, carrying their heavy quoits. But young people still enter the game, and in 1977 one of them, 11 year old Andrew White of Ugthorpe, beat 63 fellow competitors to win the Danby Open Championship. Nor is there any lack of character, as was demonstrated during a match I attended at Beck Hole. Unable to find a rag with which to clean his quoits, a Sleights player fearlessly grabbed a handful of nettles and announced, 'These will do.' Dedication to any game could surely go no further.

The Black Swan, Helmsley

'Who does not know the famous Swan?' Wordsworth's question refers to the Swan Hotel, Grasmere. But he might just as easily have asked the question about the Black Swan, Helmsley, for the inn is often associated with the poet. Wordsworth's wife-to-be, Mary Hutchinson, lived at Gallows Hill Farm, between Brompton and Wykeham, near Scarborough. When visiting her in July 1802, William and his sister Dorothy stayed overnight in Helmsley after walking across the moors from Thirsk, via Sutton Bank and Rievaulx. In her diary, Dorothy wrote: 'We reached Helmsley just at dusk. We had a beautiful view of the castle from the top of the hill, slept at a very nice inn, and were well treated.' The Black Swan is usually regarded as being this inn, although there is a rival claim for the former Golden Lion Inn, now a butcher's shop near the Market Cross.

Dorothy's praise was obviously sincere, for on 4 October of the same year she and William again called at the inn, this time with Mary. William and Mary had just been married at Brompton Parish Church, where the marriage certificate, describing Wordsworth as 'a gentleman of Grasmere', is kept in the vestry. Dorothy tells us that soon after starting out for Grasmere they spent some time in Kirbymoorside while the horses were fed. All three of them 'sauntered about' the churchyard, noting in particular a gravestone in memory of five children and another to a woman who, according to her unusual epitaph,

198

had been neglected by her relations. Dorothy's diary goes on:

> Before we reached Helmsley our driver told us that he could
> not take us any further, so we stopped at the same inn where we
> had slept before. My heart danced at the sight of its cleanly out-
> side, bright yellow walls, casements overshadowed with jasmine,
> and low, double gable-ended front . . . Mary and I warmed our-
> selves at the kitchen fire. We then walked into the garden, and
> looked over a gate, up to the old ruin which stands at the top of a
> mound, and round about it the moats are grown up into soft
> green cradles . . . I prevailed upon William to go up with me to
> the ruins. We left Mary sitting by the kitchen fire. The sun shone,
> it was warm and pleasant. One part of the castle seems to be
> inhabited. There was a man mowing nettles in the open space
> which had most likely once been the castle court. There is one
> gateway exceedingly beautiful. Children were playing upon the
> sloping ground. We came home by the street.

Was the inn to which the trio returned the Black Swan or the
Golden Lion? Situated directly opposite the castle, the Lion
seems most likely to have had such an excellent view of the ruin.
But the Lion is believed to have been a black and white tim-
bered building, whereas Dorothy describes the walls of their
pub as 'bright yellow'. In the Black Swan's favour we might
perhaps admit as evidence a visitor's account from early this
century which reveals that the pub was bedecked with flowers
in much the same manner that captivated Dorothy: the account
speaks of the hotel's 'heavy clematis wreaths of Tyrian dye',
and its 'window boxes full of scarlet geraniums'.

Whether or not the Black Swan was the Wordsworths' hotel,
it has inevitably changed a good deal since their day. It is
believed that during alterations of 1869, costing £1,620, a third
storey was added, which would remove the gabled front. Recently, an extension costing £220,000 has been skilfully grafted
on to the back of the hotel.

Apart from this extension, the hotel embraces three formerly
separate buildings. The original inn, still incorporating the
main entrance, is at one end of the block. Adjoining it is a handsome Georgian building, Bankins House. Built in 1836 to

replace a thatched cottage, it was absorbed into the hotel soon after World War II.

From 1725 until 1863, the thatched cottage and Bankins House were the home of a family named Sandwith, whose connection with Helmsley is longer than that of any other family. The achievements of various members of the family, in Law, Medicine, and the Army, are recorded on seven tablets in the parish church. About 100 years ago these tablets became the centre of a furious row involving Helmsley's redoubtable Vicar Gray (see p 166). Amid great local controversy Gray shifted the tablets to make way for new wall paintings. When the Archbishop of York heard of this, letters cannonaded between his palace and Gray's vicarage. The exchanges lasted for over a year, but the tablets remain where Gray put them—all of which helps to explain why one of the tablets can be read only with the aid of binoculars!

Between Bankins House and the churchyard is the third building incorporated into the Black Swan—Helmsley's half-timbered rectory. Before the dissolution of the monasteries in 1539, this picturesque building was the home of the rent and tithe collector of Kirkham Priory, but after that date it was taken over by the agent of the Duke of Rutland, who had large estates in the area. In 1644, when the Duke's men were besieged in the castle for three months, the house was maltreated by the opposing Parliamentarians. Although the Duke's forces held the castle for the king, the agent wrote that his home had been 'defased, outhouses pulled downe, and furnetaur taken away'. The building became part of the Black Swan in 1954.

A stagecoach service operated from the Black Swan to London. Other services included the 'Helmsley Flyer', introduced in about 1834 and making three journeys a week between Richmond, York and Helmsley. The service was later extended to Kirbymoorside.

The exact age of the hotel is unknown, but it was certainly in existence before the earliest written record of 1784. The part that the Wordsworths probably visited has yard-thick walls and adzed oak ceiling-timbers. Just inside the entrance is some fine Jacobean panelling, removed from the church when it was restored in 1860. An impressive Tudor doorway nearby is said to originate from the castle, but more likely it came from the Canon's Garth, another splendid half-timbered house behind the rectory. This noteworthy building was the original priest's home and, although not the official vicarage, it is again occupied by the vicar. An isolated dripstone in its garden wall, visible from the pavement north of the church, indicates the place where the doorway now in the Black Swan may once have stood.

Another interesting feature of the hotel is the fine wooden model of the black swan herself mounted above the entrance—'swimming life-size overhead' as a visitor once remarked. The model identifies the hotel so effectively that very few people notice the deliberate omission of the name from the inn sign.

12

FAMILIAR FEATURES

Fylingdales' Warning Station

When an incredulous North Yorkshire first learned of the proposal to build the Fylingdales' Early Warning Station, the scheme met with almost total opposition. Now, any suggestion for dismantling the station would reveal the deep gulf between those who still regard the three famous golf balls as a gross intrusion and those who see them as a fit match for the moors.

No one can doubt that the golf balls are a feature of the moors that most visitors like to see. A postcard view of them is among the region's top sellers. Suitably mounted on massive square plinths, as though about to be driven off from their own outsize golfing tees, they might even be the national park's most widely known symbol.

In my opinion, the mood of the golf balls is perfectly expressed in Sir Nikolaus Pevsner's description of them as 'the geometry of the space age at its most alluring and frightening'. To me, the ugliness of the station lies in its conventional clutter—a mess of chicken-wire fences, open radar screens and even concrete lamp-posts in the middle of the moors. I would be delighted if all this vanished tomorrow, but I also believe that when the complex becomes redundant, the three golf balls should be preserved. Further, its internal equipment should be retained and open to the public, for the warning station is part of the long history of the defence of our island, dating back through the pill boxes of two world wars to Roman forts and the earthworks of prehistoric man. When the station closes, the moors will acquire an ancient monument as striking as any in England. It requires only a little imagination to see the warning station as the twentieth century's Stonehenge—a comparison easily justified by its scale, setting and atmosphere, not to mention the puzzle it will present to a far distant age.

Most people today know that the station was built to alert the Western world of nuclear attack. The news that the station would give Britain a four-minute warning prompted a joke that one or two Britons could run a mile in that time. This was a reference to Roger Bannister's historic four-minute mile of 1954, still fresh in the public mind when Fylingdales was proposed in 1960. Of course, the strategy behind the station is that it will act as a deterrent so that the four-minute warning might never be needed. Similar stations exist at Thule in Greenland and Cleare in Alaska, and one can wonder at the speculation of future archaeologists pinpointing evidence of massive identical structures in all three of these unlikely locations. The unique trinity might become a new mystery of the universe!

The full title of the complex is the Fylingdales' Ballistic Missile Early Warning Station, abbreviated to BMEWS. The proper name for the golf balls is radomes. Each radome weighs about 100 tons and is 154ft high and 140ft in diameter—the size of a small cathedral. The domes are constructed of 1,646 laminated glass-fibre panels, some hexagonal and some pentagonal, mounted in a steel frame. They house immense swivelling radar dishes 84ft in diameter and with a range of 3,000 miles. These can detect an object as small as a tea tray floating hundreds of miles above Moscow. The station cost £45 million to build and began operating in 1964. In its first ten years it was out of commission for only twelve hours, and in the latter half of that period it was 'off the air' for an average of only ten seconds per week.

In addition to scanning for missiles, the station takes part in space missions and continuously monitors satellites and space debris. Between 1964 and 1977 the number of objects in space increased from 390 to 4,581. The number is even higher now and includes more than 900 working satellites, most of which circle the globe about every 90 minutes. So the radomes are rarely without something to look at! Their observations are logged in a computerised memory bank, listing 'all identified matter in orbit'.

Responsibility for the station, with annual running costs estimated at £2 million a few years ago, is shared between the British Government, the RAF, the USAF, and the Radio Corporation of America. In recent years there has been frequent talk of closure, usually linked with the development of 'bent radar', a system not requiring an unimpeded view and which could give a thirty-minute warning. The closure rumours have always been strongly denied, and the survival of the station, employing more than 900 people, has become an important local issue.

In summer, hundreds of people picnic by the Whitby–Pickering road at Ellerbeck Bridge in the shadow of the gleaming, misty-blue radomes. The scene of family pleasure is starkly at odds with the sombre purpose of the warning station. But it is worth anyone's effort to walk the mile or so from Ellerbeck along a track near the station's northern boundary to Lilla Howe. Here the seventh-century Lilla Cross, a symbol of early Christianity, can be seen against the background of the gently humming radomes with their overtones of nuclear war and the possible end of the world. The contrast could hardly be more complete. But I believe that even Lilla Cross would now lose something if the radomes were swept away. By their strange power to bring out the eerie qualities of the moors, the golf balls dramatically complement the landscape. Perhaps other people will agree with this view.

Roseberry Topping

Seldom a day goes by without somebody climbing Roseberry Topping's bent and battered peak. The combination of smooth slopes of grass rising to an assertive pinnacle of rock is irresistible. No hill in Yorkshire is more celebrated. At one time the Topping was probably worshipped. It has certainly been extensively quarried and mined, and even today road-stone is wrenched from a heavily gashed shoulder of the Topping at Cliff Ridge Wood. But proud Roseberry remains unbowed, and its distinctive profile, often likened to a miniature Matterhorn—but perhaps more strongly resembling a Roman nose (an emperor's of course)—issues its age-old challenge to all.

Geologically, the Topping is an 'erosional outlier'. Its cap of hard sandstone has protected the underlying shales and clays which, in the surrounding area, have been worn away to leave the Topping as a superb detached cone. The hill is almost a summary of the moors, for besides its outcrop of sandstone it has produced jet, alum-shale, moor-coal and ironstone. Near its summit is a bed of oolitic clay that makes Roseberry one of Yorkshire's classic sites for fossils: excellent specimens of leaves and ferns may be obtained with little difficulty.

In 1826, a labourer quarrying sandstone on the Topping's western flank found several apparently prehistoric implements lodged in a crevice—carved knives, a gouge, axe-heads, and an axe-mould. These may have been linked with a series of pits or shallow depressions still visible on a broad shelf of the hill above the village of Newton. Excavations early this century suggested that the pits were not dug for jet or iron since they nowhere reach the seams of these rocks. But there is evidence of hearths, and it is sometimes claimed that the pits, extending a considerable distance towards Hutton Lowcross, are the site of Roseberry's own town—an early British settlement probably centred on a fort.

Worship of the Topping perhaps began in Viking times. A clue to this lies in the earliest known form of the words Roseberry Topping—Othenesberg and Ohensberg. Found in Guisborough Priory charters of the twelfth century these are most probably derived from 'Odin's Hill', suggesting that Roseberry was sacred to the Scandinavian god.

There are other theories about the name. In Celtic, the words

205

'ros-bari' mean 'the promontory of the ship'. This could be a reference to Roseberry's usefulness as a landmark from the North Sea. Most experts agree, however, that 'Roseberry' is a mutation in common speech from the old English place named Newton-under-Ousebergh—the village at the base of the Topping. Spoken by many successive generations 'under-Ousebergh' gradually became 'Roseberry'. This name first appears in a seventeenth-century account by the topographer William Camden, and it was preceded by at least eight other forms.

From Roseberry's Viking period comes the hill's own legend, about Oswy, the infant son of a Northumbrian princess. Having dreamt that her child would drown, the princess carried him to what seemed the utterly dry slopes of the Topping. But as the princess slept the child wandered away and was drowned in an unsuspected well not far from the summit. 'Roseberry Well' is still marked on 2½in maps but is now no more than a reed-filled hollow, about 30yd north of the path between the summit and the col towards Hutton Gate.

Almost certainly among the people who have ascended the Topping is Captain James Cook, the explorer. Cook was born in 1728 at Marton near Middlesbrough and he moved with his family to Great Ayton when he was eight. His father worked at Airyholme Farm on the southern slopes of Roseberry Topping. Cook attended school in Great Ayton for five years and afterwards worked for about two years with his father on the farm.

Cook's schoolroom in Great Ayton is now a small museum, and it deserves a visit even though the premises have been rebuilt twice since Cook's day. Elsewhere in the village, an obelisk marks the site of a cottage to which Cook's parents retired in 1755. Cook is known to have visited his parents in the cottage, which was dismantled and re-erected in Melbourne, Australia, in 1934. The grave of Cook's mother and five of his brothers and sisters can be seen in the churchyard not far from the site of the cottage. Particularly worth noting on the headstone is the death of William, whose age is meticulously given as two years, twelve months, sixteen days and seven hours. The stone mason, believed by some people to have been Mr Cook himself, resolved doubts about whether the infant died in 1747 or 1748 by engraving the date thus: 174$\frac{7}{8}$.

At one time there was a suggestion for a huge statue of Captain Cook to be erected on Roseberry Topping. Better by far, since the Topping itself needs no adornment, was the placing of the Captain Cook Monument on the flat-topped Easby Hill, an immediate neighbour of the Topping. Erected in 1827 by Thomas Campion of Whitby, the monument is an obelisk 51ft high and 12ft square. By taking an inscription on the obelisk literally at its word, many guidebooks continue to inform their readers that Captain Cook was killed by natives at 'Owyhee' (simply an archaic spelling of Hawaii). The inscription records a restoration of the obelisk in 1895 but the repair of the column in 1960 after it had been split by lightning is still awaiting a mention. An excellent walk links the monument with the Topping around the rim of a low escarpment.

Although a mere 1057ft high, the Topping is still sometimes acclaimed as 'Yorkshire's highest hill'. The honour properly belongs to Whernside in the Dales—more than twice the height of the Topping. Roseberry's hold on the title is ceremonial and stems from a remark by Margery Moorpout, a fictional Cleveland countrywoman in an old dialect farce entitled *The Register Office*. Answering an inquiry about the Topping, Margery says: 'Ah thowt onny feeal hed knawn Roseberry. It's t'highest hill i' all Yorkshire. It's aboot a mahl an' a hawf heagh an' as cawd as ice at top i't'yattest day i'summer.' I have always suspected that Margery was like one or two other Yorkshire folk and knew little of any geographic feature more than a few miles from her home. She probably had not climbed Roseberry Topping since she was a child!

William Camden's account of the Topping, written as part of a book about Britain, is interesting for its reference to Roseberry as a 'prognostic of weather'. He quotes a rhyme apparently famous even then (300 years ago) and still in common use:

> When Roseberry Topping wears a cap
> Let Cleveland then beware a clap

When the local historian John Ord wrote about the hill in the early nineteenth century he testily complained that 'certain Visigoths have actually worked our classic mount as a quarry'. One can imagine his words if he had seen the hill forty years later at the height of the ironstone boom, for in the 1880s several workings were opened along the 750ft contour, soon to be followed by others lower down. At first, an aerial ropeway conveyed the ironstone to the Ayton–Middlesbrough railway, part of today's Esk Valley line. Later a narrow-gauge line was laid to the northern foot of the Topping, and there was even a proposal for a standard-gauge line, up Bousdale from the Guisborough branch. In 1912 two trains of iron-ore were despatched daily from the Topping. The mines closed in 1920, but the entrances to two old workings and the foundations of some mine buildings can be seen on the southern slopes of the hill.

Two iron posts on the top of Roseberry are probably relics of quarrying. This reduced the height of the hill and also caused the disappearance of a so-called hermitage, hollowed from a rock named Wilfred's Needle. Stone from the Topping, however, was probably used to build a pavilion, or summer house, that still stands by the path from Great Ayton. The pavilion was commissioned by Commodore Wilson, of Ayton Hall, in the eighteenth century.

At that time Roseberry also had its own bathing pool, known as Chapel Well. The water was said to be good for rheumatism and similar disorders. According to one report, the well was 'much resorted to by the youth of neighbouring villages, who assembled to drink the simple beverage and to join in a variety of rural diversions'. Eventually, however, the water was diverted to a drain and the bath house demolished. But the place can still be seen—a marshy area in a field adjoining Cliff Ridge Wood, with the bed of the former narrow-gauge railway not far away.

At dusk, one day in November 1971, passers-by on the Newton Road might have noticed mounted huntsmen very near the summit of the Topping. A fox, raised a mile or two away at Nunthorpe, took refuge among the topmost crags. The master and first whip rode to within twenty yards of the Ord-nance column before conceding defeat. This was a remarkable repeat of a hunt of 6 April 1843, when a Guisborough hunts-man, Thomas Parrington, noted in his journal that a fox 'took shelter in a creek of rock on the very summit of Roseberry . . . Should I hunt all my days it is a thousand to one I shall ever see a fox run to the top of far-famed Roseberry.'

Unfortunately, the view from far famed Roseberry is not what it used to be. The moorland panorama to the south, with Cook's monument prominent, is still superb. But the destruc-tion of trees and hedgerows, coupled with the intrusion of large farm buildings and the advance of the Teesside suburbs, is making the plain of Cleveland very dog-eared. In April 1974 the Topping was partially severed from Great Ayton—an act as unpardonable as divorcing Coniston from its Old Man. While Ayton remains proudly in North Yorkshire, half of the Topping is now within the new County of Cleveland, which bears only a token resemblance to the historic region of the same name. And even though the old boundaries hold good for all sentimental and some practical purposes, the glum truth is that Roseberry Topping has become part of a 'borough' that also contains sev-eral of Teesside's most heavily populated towns, and a large slice of the region's vast steel, oil, and chemical industries.

Very close at hand the speculative estates of Guisborough and Great Ayton reach towards the Topping, and it is not too far-fetched to foresee the day when this fine hill will rise from a plinth of bungalows and command a view mainly of urban sprawl. This should be prevented—but the best time to climb Roseberry Topping is today.

The White Horse

White Horse spotting is a favourite sport of all Yorkshiremen. Naturally, the game is confined to the county's own horse, at Kilburn in the North York Moors. Any claim of an unusual sighting is the signal for every Yorkshireman—and woman—

who has ever seen the horse to rush in with their own most distant or novel glimpse of the creature.

My furthest sighting of the horse is a mere 19 miles, from the central tower of York Minster and from the nearby city walls. But if we can accept the evidence of a particularly lively correspondence to *The Dalesman* in 1971–2, the White Horse can be seen from Brimham Rocks in the Yorkshire Dales and Leavening Brow in the Wolds (both 21 miles); from Wike Cross between Leeds and Harrogate, and from Greenhow Hill between Pately Bridge and Grassington (both 27 miles); from Brayton Barff near Selby (34 miles); from Queensbury, west of Bradford (41 miles); and from a point on the Doncaster road 6 miles south of Pontefract (43 miles).

Close to his own pastures, the horse can be seen from so many places in and around Harrogate that it is a wonder he has never been adopted as the town's mascot. Rarer sightings are from two points in Leeds—the Cookridge Water Tower and the GPO mast at Tinshill, the highest point in the city. An observer from Tinshill told *The Dalesman* that the White Horse was a reliable barometer across a distance of 30 miles: a clear view of him after a warm day meant rain in the next 24 hours.

No doubt the White Horse's creators would be overjoyed to know he has become such a firm Yorkshire favourite. The Kilburn horse is the most northerly in Britain, and unlike most of his companions he is not prehistoric. The idea for making him is said to have been suggested in the late eighteenth or early nineteenth century by Thomas Taylor of Kilburn, when he returned from a visit to the White Horse at Uffington, Berkshire. His idea was not adopted, but about half a century later it was revived by John Hodgson, Kilburn's schoolmaster. It was he and fellow villagers who cut the horse on the 1–4 escarpment overlooking the Vale of York. An old postcard notes that on the day the task was completed, 4 November 1857, thirty-three men were at work on the horse.

During the project two scale drawings of the horse were used—one on the site and the other in the village as a means of arranging and checking the work. The first of these drawings is now preserved in the Yorkshire Museum, York. Until 1977, when it was sold at an auction, the second drawing was displayed in the 'Mouseman' furniture showrooms at Kilburn. Both drawings are by Hodgson, on the scale of 3in to 100ft.

In true Victorian fashion the horse is a straightforward representation: none of the figurative fancies of early man. But the horse's vital statistics are impressive. At 314ft long and 228ft high he is much larger than any of the ancient horses. To fence him in completely would enclose 2 acres of moor. About twenty people can stand on the grass island that forms his eye—but walking on the horse is strongly discouraged.

The horse-racing history of the Hambleton Hills (see p 215) makes the horse an appropriate symbol in this part of the moors. But the Kilburn horse needs more grooming than most. While the ancient horses are cut firmly into limestone or chalk, the Kilburn horse is inadequately pastured on shifting clay and light soil. Originally, 6 tons of lime were used to whiten him, and weathering and erosion means that the job frequently has to be redone. The work is carried out by the Kilburn White Horse Association, a registered charity whose aim is 'to preserve and maintain the horse for public benefit'. In the 1960s the association organised the biggest ever restoration of the horse. His shape was recut and stabilised, drainage channels were dug, and a new coat of chalk applied. The association also cleaned and relettered Hodgson's gravestone in Kilburn churchyard.

Since then an aerial survey has been carried out, and in 1974 the association estimated that the weekly cost of keeping the horse in good fettle was £12. His weakest features are his fetlocks, which become ragged or non-existent. His hindquarters, too, often seem only tenuously attached to his body. The persistent difficulty in remedying these and other imperfections is why the temptation to stand on the horse, if only for a moment or two, must be resisted. In 1976, to improve access, an old flight of steps alongside the horse was improved, and these are now part of an official 1½-mile White Horse Walk created by the Forestry Commission.

Although duty demands that all Yorkshire folk must visit their county's horse at least once in their lifetime, the creature is undoubtedly better seen from a distance. I believe that the finest view is from the York–Thirsk road north of Easingwold. But, as the eagerness to take part in White Horse spotting confirms, it is a pleasure to catch a glimpse of the horse from anywhere. Yorkshire's White Horse might not be much of a thoroughbred but he is well loved.

The Drove Road

As a prominent man-made track with its own distinctive history the Drove Road is to the west of the North York Moors what the Roman Road is to the east, although more scenic. Its finest stretch forms a breezy ridgeway along the full length of Black Hambleton, a massive but sharply defined hill berthed like a *Titanic* among more rolling moors. Away towards Hawnby are the rich woods of Arden Hall and Upper Ryedale, while in the opposite direction lie the quiet meadows and little known byways around Nether Silton, Over Silton, and Kepwick. It is all delectable countryside, with the Drove Road as its splendid centrepiece.

Altogether the road runs for about 15 miles within the national park. Some parts have been metalled, but about 6 miles of the road are as the drovers of the eighteenth and early nineteenth centuries would have known it—a broad green track curling along the crest of the moors. Water drains quickly into the limestone that underlies most of the 'road', so that walking here is often dry when other moorland paths are a quagmire.

The road is much older than the droving from which it now takes its name. As part of an ancient route between London and Scotland, it pre-dates the North Yorkshire section of the Great North Road. Some people say the track is prehistoric. William the Conqueror is believed to have travelled along it during his harrying of the North in 1069. There is little doubt that in the same century the bones of St Cuthbert, which for a time were kept at Crayke where he founded a monastery, were carried along the road to their final resting place in Durham Cathedral. In 1322, Edward II, fleeing after a disastrous Scottish campaign, was defeated in a battle against Robert Bruce at a place still called Scotch Corner, by the Drove Road near Oldstead. It is also likely that John Wesley used the road during his travels in the North of England.

Droving itself dates back to at least medieval days, but the large-scale droving that has coloured the history of this moorland route did not begin until the eighteenth century, when there was a dramatic increase in the population of London. To feed the crowded millions, about 100,000 cattle and 750,000 sheep arrived at Smithfield Market each year. It is recorded that in a single year, 28,551 cattle passed over Wetherby Bridge, most no doubt having been driven along the moorland Drove Road. Often the processions of animals stretched for 2 miles.

The drovers had regular stopping places, known as 'stances'. One of these was near Limekiln House, now a ruin on the east side of the Drove Road above Kepwick. The building was once an inn, and in 1960 I met Luke Kendall, a shepherd whose family once lived there. He remembered driving sheep along the Drove Road to Swainby sheep sale between the two world wars. He told me that before his family occupied the house it was the home of a family called Cowton. There is a story that when the Cowtons moved they took with them a goose, sitting on eggs in a clothes' basket! A bonfire was burned at Limekiln House to mark the golden jubilee of Queen Victoria's reign in 1877, but the house has never been inhabited during this century.

Appropriately enough, the old Scotch Corner battlefield (not to be confused with Scotch Corner on the A1) is today the site of a chapel. This was created in the 1950s from a ruined farm-building by John Bunting, a notable North Yorkshire sculptor. The chapel is dedicated to the dead of World War II, and in particular to three former pupils of Ampleforth College—Hugh Dormer, Michael Fenwick, and Michael Allmand. After being twice parachuted into enemy territory, Dormer, 27, was killed

213

in the struggle for Europe in 1944. Allmand, 23, who died in the same campaign, was posthumously awarded the vc. Fenwick, 21, was killed at Kowloon, China. The chapel contains a sculpted figure by Bunting—a full-size likeness of a recumbent soldier. There are also several carvings outside the chapel, which is cared for by pupils of Ampleforth College. It is not normally open to the public but memorial services are occasionally held there. Another piece of sculpture by Bunting, dated 1969, is built into the gable wall of a lonely farm in the tiny valley of Ladhill Beck north of Hawnby.

Not far from the memorial chapel, and easily visited on an expedition to the Drove Road, is another reminder of World War II. A plaque in the porch of Scawton church records the names of five French airmen who died when their Halifax bomber crashed as it returned to Elvington, near York, after a raid on Hamburg on 17 March 1945. The plaque was formerly fixed to a tree against which the plane came to rest after crashing through two stone walls. Ironically, the five who died had all baled out and two crew members who were still in the plane when it crashed survived the ordeal. Apparently there was insufficient time for the parachutes to open.

A building that attracts attention near the Drove Road at Oldstead is a tower on a hill above the village. This is Sneverdale Observatory, erected to mark the start of Queen Victoria's reign. Originally containing a large telescope and other astronomical equipment, the building is kept permanently locked. Among several large tablets, two of which commemorate the builder of the observatory and the man who suggested it should be built (John Wormald), is one bearing a long verse that includes this couplet:

> See rich industry smiling on the plains
> And peace and plenty tell Victoria reigns.

Industry at that time, of course, still largely meant the patient tillage of the land—and happily this is still principally the prospect from the tower.

For about 200 years the grassy uplands bordering the Drove Road near Sutton Bank were used as a racecourse. In the seventeenth century the course was regarded as the Newmarket of the North, regularly attracting royal patronage. The course's isolation led to its gradual decline, with the principal event, the Queen Anne Plate, being transferred to York in 1755.

Today, however, racehorses are still trained on the old gallops, from professional stables near the Hambleton Hotel. Certain tumuli near the Cleave Dyke have retained their racehorse-era nickname of 'grooms' stools'. Most interesting is the survival in a dry-stone wall at Dialstone Farm of a flat-topped circular stone on which was placed the dial, or weighing machine, for weighing-in the jockeys.

By an old track that emerges on to the Drove Road from Thirlby there is also an old stone trough known as the Jennet Well, a Jennet being a kind of horse. Packhorses might well have preceded racehorses in using this well, the waters of which also became locally renowned for their supposed medicinal properties: seventy or eighty years ago children arrived in wagonettes to drink the water as a precaution against whooping-cough.

The Drove Road reaches its highest point at 1257ft on Black Hambleton. The Cleveland Way, one of Britain's official long-distance footpaths, follows the road here, having joined it at High Paradise Farm near Boltby. On the steep descent of Black Hambleton's northern shoulder the walk passes the remains of a lime-kiln. A short metalled stretch of road is then reached, notable for a wayside farm named Chequers. Like Limekiln House this was once an inn. The faded motto can still be read:

Be not in haste—step in and taste
Ale tomorrow for nothing.

Cattle were shod before their journey along the Drove Road, and smithies specialising in the work sprang up along the route. It is also said that geese and turkeys—which made the inevitable Christmas journey along the Drove Road—sometimes had felt pads fitted to their feet or were made to paddle through a compound of tar, sawdust and sand before beginning their trek. Pigs, too, were herded along the Drove Road, but without special footwear.

The drovers themselves were nomads. Many came from Scotland, which perhaps explains why names such as Scotland Nook and Scotland Farm appear near the Drove Road. There is also a Bawderis Wood, which might be a corruption of Borderers.

Travelling between 10 and 14 miles each day the drovers included a 'topsman', whose job was to go ahead and make arrangements for the following night. The drovers drank whisky from rams' horns and ate oatmeal and onions, sometimes mixed with animal blood to form a kind a black pudding. They had dogs that lived on beer and bread and sometimes ran unaccompanied back to Scotland. When the drovers were returning home, with money in exchange for their livestock, they faced the ever-present threat of robbery—a hazard reflected in the Drove Road's alternative name, the Thieves' Highway.

An early blow to droving was the development of canning, introduced as long ago as the early nineteenth century. The expanding railway network soon left most drovers high and dry, and their work finally ceased with the advent of refrigeration, which eliminated the need even to send cattle to slaughterhouses in the nearest town. From then on, animals were slaughtered locally and the meat itself was distributed. Although some local droving lingered into the twentieth century, long-distance work petered out rapidly after about 1850. In 1961, the man believed to be the last surviving drover celebrated his 100th birthday in Yorkshire. At Thirsk the great days of droving are charmingly recalled by a cast-iron milepost bearing the legend 'London 220 miles' and the figure of a drover with one of his beasts. But pleasing though this well known curiosity is, it was almost certainly manufactured long after droving had passed its peak.

Sutton Bank and Gormire

Sutton Bank and Gormire form a peculiar partnership, for while the bank is usually heavy with petrol fumes and loud with the clash of gears, Gormire hides herself away, a reluctant jewel in the national park crown. And yet by name Gormire is probably as well known as the nearby bank, her fame assured by her role as one of Yorkshire's only two natural lakes, the other being Semerwater in Wensleydale.

The formation of Gormire goes back to the Ice Age, when a glacier in the Vale of York pressed hard against the edge of the moors. As it moved south, it steadily eroded the spur of moorland on which Gormire now lies. The basin containing the lake might have been gouged by the glacier as part of the erosion process, or it might have been scooped out later by water surging around the glacier as the ice began to melt. Either way, the northern end of the basin was ultimately blocked by a deposit of mud torn from the cliffs by the swirling water. With the southern outlet already barred by a resistant ridge of rock, Gormire came into being—a tarn-like lake on an unexpected shelf 500ft below the rim of the moors. The seclusion of the setting is increased by the broad-leaved woods that crowd to the water's edge almost all round the lake. And although thousands of people enjoy the bird's eye view of Gormire from the top of Sutton Bank, not too many relish the steep walk down to the shore and back again. So, for the present, Gormire remains a shy stretch of water, the haunt of coot and the Great-crested Grebe, occasionally visited by deer, and the home of a particularly fine colony of bulrushes.

The moorland background is exceptionally grand. Only a mile or so away is the bull-nosed cliff of Roulston Scar. From there, the escarpment swerves round to Gormire as a huge concave bowl. This helps to funnel the prevailing south-westerly wind, giving splendid uplift to the gliders of the Yorkshire Gliding Club, which has its headquarters at Sutton Bank.

Towering immediately above Gormire is the shattered 70ft Whitestone Cliff. In strong sunshine its gleaming sandstone face becomes almost as prominent a landmark as Kilburn's White Horse. John Wesley visited the village of Sutton-under-Whitestone Cliff shortly after a massive fall of rock from the cliff on 25 March 1755. Wesley's account of the fall says that the first indications came at about 7am when men working near the cliff heard 'a roaring like many cannon'. He goes on: 'It seemed to come from the cliffs . . . They saw a large body of stone, four or five yards broad, split and fly off from the very top of the rocks.' According to Wesley the ground shook and trembled for the next two days with rocks still rolling down. 'The earth also clave asunder in very many places,' he declares.

William and Dorothy Wordsworth also visited this neighbourhood on their journey in July 1802 to William's future wife, Mary, at Brompton, near Scarborough. In her journal Dorothy notes that when they told their landlady at Thirsk that they intended to walk over Sutton Bank she 'threw out some saucy words in our hearing'. Dorothy adds: 'The day was very hot and we rested often and long before we reached the foot of the Hamilton (Hambleton) Hills and while we were climbing them still oftener.' With Mary, the Wordsworths made the same journey in the opposite direction in October. It was dusk when they reached the top of Sutton Bank, and Dorothy records:

> 'We had not wanted fair prospects before us as we drove along the flat plain of the high hill. Far far off us in the western sky we saw the shapes of castles, ruins among groves, a great spreading wood, rocks and single trees, a minster with its tower unusually distinct, minarets in another quarter, and a round Grecian temple . . . As we decended the hill there was no distinct view but of a great space; only near us we saw the wild and (as people say) bottomless tarn . . . it seemed to be made visible only by its own light, for all the hill about us was dark.

Dorothy concludes that arriving in Thirsk 'the landlady was quite civil. She did not recognise the despised foot travellers.'

The belief that Gormire is bottomless is one of many legends about the lake. But the view from Sutton Bank reveals quite clearly that much of the lake is shallow. The bed can be traced up to about 50yd from the shore. Several large boulders visible beneath the surface could be from the rock-fall noted by Wesley.

There is little doubt, however, that the lake was once much deeper than it is now, for terraces marking two earlier shore lines can be traced around much of the lake. The oldest terrace is more than 15ft above the present level of the lake. Unless there was once a sizeable stream that has since disappeared, enough water to fill the lake to this level could have come only from the melting Vale of York glacier. The steep slope immediately below the terrace is also consistent with a retreating glacier, suggesting a rapid fall in the water level.

The second terrace is only about 8ft above today's lake level. Very interestingly, it runs across a landslip at the foot of Whitestone Cliff. This might indicate that the slip, perhaps part of the great collapse of 1755, stemmed the fall in the water level. Since then, however, the lake has continued to decrease in size, its shoreline now varying from between 10ft and 20ft inside the second terrace.

The wonder is that the lake exists at all, for no streams run either in or out. Although an unknown spring might rise in the lake bed, most experts believe that the lake is sustained only by direct rainfall and water draining from the moors. On the eastern shore a shallow channel takes the overflow in time of flood, but even there the water quickly sinks into the ground rather than running away as a stream.

Putting geology aside, there is a folklore version of the origin of Gormire in which the Devil, riding a white horse, leapt from the top of the hill and vanished into the earth. The hole he created slowly filled with water to become Gormire. There is also a rhyme that says:

> When Gormire riggs shall be clothed with hay
> The White mare of Whissoncliff [Whitestone Cliff] will bear it away.

This white mare has nothing to do with Kilburn's White Horse, although the many stories about the Whitestone Cliff mare might have played a part in the decision to cut the hillside

219

horse. A favourite tale is that the white mare bolted with its rider over the cliff into Gormire, where the rider can still be heard grooming the horse each midnight. Another tale tells of how an abbot of Rievaulx challenged a knight to a race along the cliffs. The knight borrowed a white horse from the abbot who promptly forced both horse and rider over the precipice. As the knight fell to his death, he noticed that the abbot resembled the Devil.

Gormire is poorly served by rights of way but a public path skirts the southern edge of the lake and a bridleway touches the shore at the overflow point. By the steepest part of the path between there and Sutton Bank is one of the moorland Windy Pits—a series of limestone fissures found mainly in the Ryedale area. In 1953 a thirteen year old boy scrambling in a Windy Pit near Helmsley picked up an ancient beaker. Together with later discoveries, this proved to be important evidence that the beaker people of the late Bronze Age—so-called because they customarily placed a beaker in their burial mounds—were more strongly established in the moors than had previously been thought.

Between Gormire Windy Pit and the lake stands a huge block of stone, estimated to weigh 20 tons. A curious mark on the top, resembling a human foot, has led some people to suggest that that stone was once the scene of human sacrifices. A more homely feature a short distance through the woods is a small quarry that yielded the soft sandstone formerly used for burnishing steps and window-sills. It was known as hearthstone or donkey stone, and large quantities were taken from Gormire to the West Riding by horse and cart.

Most of the motorists who today coax their vehicles up Sutton Bank are probably unaware of all this history so close at hand. Likely to be imprinted on their minds, however, is the knowledge of Sutton Bank as one of Yorkshire's great motoring hills. With its 1–4 gradient and double hairpin bend it was once the scene of motor-bike trials. A hazard in those days were large lumps of rock protruding from the road. One day a steam roller overturned, and during the recovery operation workmen discovered a cavity beneath the road large enough to contain the entire vehicle: two of Sutton Bank's infamous rocks had prevented the roller from crashing through.

Almost a mile long, Sutton Bank continues to catch many motorists unawares. One Saturday in July 1977 five breakdown wagons were engaged on the bank for most of the day: once no fewer than thirty stranded vehicles awaited their attention.

Luckily, the bank remained free of such incidents a month earlier despite the presence of thousands of people for the lighting of one of the 103 bonfires in the official chain to celebrate the Queen's Silver Jubilee. The fire was lit on sight of the blaze on Otley Chevin and it passed the signal on to Wensleydale's Penhill, from where the chain extended both northwards into County Durham and eastwards to Turkey Nab near Ingleby Greenhow, a second bonfire site within the moors. I was present at the Turkey Nab blaze, when champagne toasts were drunk, 'Ilkley Moor Baht 'At' was sung, and a marvellous occasion was enjoyed by all.

In a fenced enclosure just off Sutton Bank is a plaque marking a Bronze Age burial. Beyond it rises the conical peak of Hood Hill, detached from the escarpment by only a few hundred yards. In common with several less obvious outliers, occurring mainly between Sutton Bank and Thimbleby, the hill is believed to have been shaped by water eddying between the retreating Vale of York glacier and the escarpment. Some very recent research has suggested that a castle might once have crowned the hill. A more fairy-tale-like situation would be hard to imagine, but although written records of the castle have been traced up to 1322 no evidence of any building has yet been found.

It is impossible not to wonder, however, whether Hood Hill Castle was the inspiration for yet another local legend, about a knight who returned from the Crusades and built a castle in which to imprison his faithless mistress. The castle was later submerged in a flood but it supposedly still stands beneath the still silent waters of Gormire. If so, it will no doubt be a busy place, sheltering all those ghostly horses and riders.

ACKNOWLEDGEMENTS

Although the material for this book has been especially written some of the items are based on articles by me that first appeared in *The Northern Echo* and *The Dalesman*. These have been extensively revised, with much new matter added, but I am very grateful indeed to Mr Don Evans, Editor of *The Northern Echo*, and Mr Bill Mitchell, Editor of *The Dalesman*, for readily allowing me to make fresh use of material prepared originally for their publications.

I am also grateful to Mr Ronald Scriven for permission to reproduce his poem 'Kirkdale,' on pp 145–6, and to the publishers of the following works for allowing me to quote extracts that appear in my text on the pages mentioned: *Duel of Eagles* by Peter Townsend (Weidenfeld & Nicolson, 1970), on pp 90–1; *Yorkshire: The North Riding* (Buildings of England Series) by Sir Nikolaus Pevsner (Penguin Books, 1966), on pp 146 and 185; *North Eastern Steam* by W. A. Tuplin (George Allen and Unwin, 1970), on p 134; *Queen of the Dales* by George Harland (Ruth Fletcher, of Glaisdale, 1970), on p 139; *The Ryedale Historian*, 1974 (Helmsley and District Archaeology Society), on p 185. The photocopy of the engraving of Whitby lifeboat on p 67 appears by permission of the *Illustrated London News*.

For the modern black-and-white photographs I am indebted to: *The Evening Gazette*, Middlesbrough, Nos 6, 8, 9, 14; Paul Hines of York, No 10; *The Northern Echo*, Darlington, Nos 11, 12; Colin Simister of Darlington, Nos 4, 7, 13; Simon Warner of

Stanbury, near Keighley, Nos 1, 2, 3.

I particularly wish to thank Mrs Jessie Fearne, of York, for permission to use a colour transparency by her late son Lawrie as the cover illustration. Above all, my thanks must go to my wife not only for her skill in typing the manuscript but for her encouragement during the five years it took me to prepare and write this book.

INDEX

Numbers in italic type indicate illustrations

Ainhowe Cross, 28
Ainsley family, 191-2, 194
Aislaby, 78
alum, 54-9, 65, 171, 205
Ampleforth, 19, 23; college, 30-1, 213-14
Appleton-le-Moors, 39
Arden Hall, 53, 212
Atkinson, Canon J.C., 34, 35, 71, 113-14, 121

Barry, Sir Charles, 183
Battersby, 118, 126, 138, 139, 140
Baxter, George, 39-40
Beadlam, 98, 99, 170, 172, 180
Beck Hole, 52, *101*, 134, 136, 195, 197, 198
Beckett, Sir Martyn, 185
Beggar's Bridge, 69-72
Belcher, Henry, 135
Bell Pits, 51, 103
Bell, Richard, 105
Betjeman, Sir John, 145

Bilsdale: Ainsley family, 191-2, 194; Canon Kyle, 161; daffodils, 104; Dowson, Bobby, 192-3; hunt, 192-3; jet, 64; linear earthwork, 21-2; memorial stone, 111; origin of name, 22; rare bird found, 121; Spout House, *119*, 190-5; watercourse, 98; Weatherill family, 61, 111, 194-5, see also Tripsdale
birds, 15, 118-19, 217
Black Hambleton, 212, 215
Black Swan, 198-201
Blakey Ridge, 14, 24, 26, 40, 43, 109, 127
Blakey Topping, 76
Blowith, 125, 129-30
Bonfield Gill, 98, 100
Botton Hall, 118
Boulby, 55-6, 57
Bousdale, 208
Bransdale, 98, 109, 144, 145, 167, 195
Brompton, 19, 36, 37, 38, 164, 198
Bronze Age, 14-15, 23, 220, 221
Bulmer Stone, *102*, 112-13

225